# Gourmet Ireland 2

As Seen on Public Television

# Gourmet Ireland 2

Paul and Jeanne Rankin

San Francisco

**Note for Vegetarians:**

Recipes suitable for vegetarians are marked with a (V) symbol. Please note that these may include cheese and other dairy products.



First published by BBC Books. North American Edition published 1998 by Bay Books & Tapes, Inc., by arrangement with BBC Books, an imprint of BBC Worldwide Publishing.

This book is published to accompany the second *Gourmet Ireland* television series. Executive Producer: Brian Waddell. Director: Stephen Stewart.

For information, address:
Bay Books & Tapes, 555 De Haro St., Suite 220, San Francisco, CA 94107.

*Publisher:* James Connolly
*Art Director:* Jeffrey O'Rourke
*Editor for the North American Edition:* Sharon Silva
*Book and Cover Design:* Shelly Meadows/Homefire
*Production:* Kristen Wurz
*Proofreader:* Sabrina Rood-Sinker

Bay Books may be purchased for education, business, or sales promotional use at attractive quantity discounts. Please contact Bay Books & Tapes/555 De Haro St., Suite 220/San Francisco, CA 94107.

Library of Congress Cataloguing-in-Publication Data

Rankin, Paul.
Gourmet Ireland 2 / Paul and Jeanne Rankin.
"As seen on public television."
Originally published: London: BBC. 1995.
Includes index.
ISBN 0-912333-34-0
1. Cookery, Irish. 2. Gourmet Ireland (Television program)
I. Rankin, Jeanne. II. Gourmet Ireland (Television program)
III. Title.
TX717.5.R36 1998
641.59417--dc21 97-46795
CIP

ISBN 0-912333-34-0

Printed in China

10 9 8 7 6 5 4 3 2 1

Distributed to the trade by Publishers Group West

# Contents

Acknowledgments

We would like to thank our producer, **Brian Waddell,** and our director, **Stephen Stewart,** for their encouragement and direction during the making of the second *Gourmet Ireland* television series. All of the film crew were absolutely wonderful.

Our admiration for the **artisans of this island** and gratitude for all that they are doing in the name of food is hard to put into words. There are so many individuals doing such amazing things. All we can say is keep it up. Your work is noticed and appreciated.

We also want to mention photographer **Graham Kirk** and his stylist, **Helen Payne.** They have done a terrific job on both books and are a real pleasure to work with.

And, of course, once again we want to thank **the staff members** back at **Roscoff**, our restaurant in Belfast. We could never have done this without their hard work and support.

**P & JR**

# Introduction

When we were traveling around Ireland for the first series of *Gourmet Ireland*, we discovered many exciting people who were growing and creating all sorts of delicious food products, both traditional and alternative. On our journey for the second series, we found that these artisans were growing in number and in knowledge. How could we not be inspired? There is a wealth of fresh produce, healthy crops, truly organic game, and bountiful fish and seafood in the country waiting to be enjoyed. Irish food will not stand still. Just as American cuisine has embraced exciting seasonings and new cooking techniques and concepts in its resurgence, so Irish food is evolving all the time. We believe that in a few years' time it will be totally accepted, in the same way that British food prepared with British products has been.

For many of us, it's only when there is a special occasion to celebrate, or when we have some friends to entertain, that we really make time to put together an appealing three-course meal. We've created these menus for just those sorts of occasion. We also, however, chose them as showcases for the tremendous products that you can find in Ireland. As a result, some of them are a little one-sided, so you should feel absolutely free to mix and match. You can liven up a Lean Times menu by including a hearty dish from Country Fare, or add some indulgence from Cupid's Cuisine to a Family Get-Together. You can also, of course, try out individual dishes. Remember, though, that you should always be guided by what's in season and by what's in your cupboard.

This book reflects one of our own particular interests, which is healthy eating. Today there is much more awareness of what foods actually do to and for us than there was in the past, and there is a much greater demand for nutritional information. People want light meals that are both good for them and easy to prepare. Vegetarianism is rapidly growing in popularity, while red-meat eaters are turning more to white meat and other lean alternatives than before.

Healthy eating doesn't have to mean a strict regime, nor does it mean cutting out natural foods like cream and butter. It's all a question of balance. Natural products, treated respectfully, will always be better for you than processed foodstuffs. The cooking method—for example, deep-fat frying or steaming—can make or break the healthfulness of a meal. Although there are a few decadent dishes in the following chapters—and everyone should feel free to indulge themselves without guilt sometimes—most of the ideas tend to go in a healthier direction. So if you find these dishes fresh, tasty and interesting, then you can be pretty sure that they are good for you, too.

CHAPTER ONE

# Catch of the Day

Ireland, surrounded by the ocean and with lakes and rivers teeming with fish, is one of the best places on earth to enjoy fish and seafood dishes. But wherever you live, find a trusty fishmonger and then try out some of these recipes.

Menu 1

Smoked Eel Pâté with Fresh Herbs

Roast Fillet of Turbot with Potato Scales

Warm Leek Vinaigrette

Chocolate Roulade with Raspberries

Menu 2

Risotto Molly Malone

Steamed Hake
with Sliced Tomatoes and Tarragon

Roast Bananas with Waffles

# Smoked Eel Pâté
## with Fresh Herbs

CONSIDERING HOW POPULAR EELS ARE ON THE CONTINENT AND THE MANY DELICIOUS WAYS THEY CAN BE COOKED, WE FIND IT AMAZING THAT MOST FOLK IN IRELAND SEEM TO BE SCARED TO DEATH OF THEM. PERHAPS IT'S THEIR SNAKELIKE APPEARANCE—HOW COULD SOMETHING THAT LOOKS LIKE THAT TASTE GOOD? WE THINK THEY'RE GREAT, AND THIS PÂTÉ WOULD MAKE A FINE RECIPE FOR CONVERTING ANY NON-BELIEVERS. SERVE IT WITH TOAST OR DELICIOUS IRISH WHOLE-WHEAT BREAD (SEE PAGE 89). IF YOU CAN'T FIND SMOKED EEL, THIS RECIPE WORKS BEAUTIFULLY WITH SMOKED MACKEREL. **Serves 6 to 8**

**2 1/2 pounds whole smoked eels or 1 1/4 pounds smoked eel fillets**

**2/3 cup unsalted butter, softened**

**1 tablespoon Dijon mustard**

**2 tablespoons chopped fresh parsley**

**2 tablespoons snipped fresh chives**

**2 tablespoons chopped fresh dill**

**1 tablespoon small capers, rinsed**

**6 tablespoons lemon juice**

**1/4 teaspoon cayenne pepper**

**1 hard-boiled egg yolk**

**salt and freshly ground black pepper**

**salad leaves to garnish (optional)**

To skin a whole eel, simply break off the head, pulling backward and downward. Don't separate the head from the skin but pull the skin down and off with the head. Locate the central bone and run a knife or your fingers between the eel flesh and the bone. Continue until the eels are completely filleted. You should have about 1 1/4 pounds of eel fillets.

Roughly chop the eel flesh and divide into two equal piles. Put one pile in a blender or food processor with the butter, mustard, herbs, capers, lemon juice, cayenne and egg yolk and process until smooth. Taste for seasoning and add salt and pepper as necessary. Scrape the eel butter into a clean bowl and mix in the remaining chopped eel. The pâté is now finished and can be spooned into ramekins or a pâté dish.

Alternatively we like to form a roll with plastic wrap (or aluminum foil). To do this, simply spread the plastic wrap on a flat surface and spoon the pâté onto one end to form a large sausage shape. Roll the pâté in the plastic wrap to make a neat cylinder and twist the ends to seal it tightly. Chill the pâté for at least 2 hours before serving. Cut into small slices and garnish with salad leaves.

# Roast Fillet of Turbot
## with Potato Scales

WHEN WE FIRST STARTED COOKING FISH WITH POTATO SCALES IT SEEMED HILARIOUS AND VERY IRISH INDEED. THIS DISH HAS A BEAUTIFUL CONTRAST OF TEXTURES AND, SERVED WITH WARM LEEK VINAIGRETTE (SEE PAGE 12), IS LIGHT YET TASTY AND SATISFYING. **Serves 6 to 8**

**6 to 8 baby potatoes**

**salt and freshly ground white pepper**

**2 tablespoons unsalted butter, melted**

**6 thick turbot fillets, about 5 ounces each**

**all-purpose flour for dredging**

**1 1/2 tablespoons vegetable oil**

**Warm Leek Vinaigrette (see page 12) to serve**

Slice the potatoes as thinly as possible (about 1/8 inch) using a sharp knife or a vegetable slicer (mandoline). Season them lightly with salt, cover with a damp cloth and allow to stand for 5 minutes. After this time you will notice that the potatoes have given off plenty of water and are limp and pliable. Pat the potato slices dry, then pour over them about 2/3 cup of the melted butter, stirring to coat the potatoes in butter. Season the fish fillets with salt and pepper, dredge lightly in flour and place on a plate. Arrange the potato slices on one side of the fillets, overlapping them slightly to give the effect of fish scales. When all the fillets are covered, chill them for at least 30 minutes to allow the potato scales to stick firmly.

Preheat the oven to 350°F.

To cook the fish, heat a large, heavy-based, ovenproof frying pan over medium heat. Add the oil and remaining butter and heat until the butter is foaming. Carefully place the fillets in the pan potato-side down and cook for about 3 minutes, or until the potatoes are beginning to brown nicely. Turn the fillets and cook for about 30 seconds to seal the other side, then turn the fish again and place the pan in the oven for 5 minutes, or until the fillets are cooked and firm to the touch.

To serve, carefully turn the fillets onto warmed plates and surround with the Warm Leek Vinaigrette.

# Warm Leek Vinaigrette

THIS IS A DELICIOUS VINAIGRETTE THAT WILL GO WELL WITH FISH, CHICKEN OR VEGETABLE DISHES.

**Serves 6 to 8** 

**3 tablespoons unsalted butter**

**3/4 cup plus 2 tablespoons water**

**1 pound leeks, thinly sliced**

**salt and freshly ground white pepper**

**6 plum tomatoes, peeled, seeded and diced**

**4 1/2 tablespoons white wine vinegar**

**2 teaspoons whole-grain mustard**

**3/4 cup plus 2 tablespoons light olive oil**

In a large pan, melt the butter with the water over high heat. Add the leeks and a little salt and cook for about 5 minutes, stirring frequently. Add the tomatoes and a few twists of pepper and remove from the heat.

In a small bowl, whisk together the wine vinegar, mustard, 1/4 teaspoon of salt and some freshly ground pepper. Whisk in the oil, then check and adjust the seasoning to taste. Add the leek mixture to the vinaigrette and serve while still warm.

# Chocolate Roulade with Raspberries

THIS DESSERT IS LIKE A SWISS ROLL, BUT THE RICHNESS OF THE CHOCOLATE SPONGE AND THE FRESH, DELICATE FLAVOR OF THE RASPBERRIES ELEVATES IT TO THE WINNER'S CIRCLE. EVERYONE WILL RETURN FOR SECONDS, SO BE PREPARED! YOU CAN SERVE THE ROULADE WITH EXTRA RASPBERRY SAUCE (SEE PAGE 80) IF YOU LIKE. **Serves 6 to 8**

**6 eggs, separated**

**2 1/4 cups confectioners' sugar, sifted**

**1 1/3 cups cocoa powder**

**1/4 cup cornstarch**

**1 1/2 cups whipping cream**

**1/4 cup superfine sugar**

**1 teaspoon vanilla extract**

**7 tablespoons raspberry jam**

**2 tablespoons water**

**1 pint (2 cups) fresh raspberries**

**fresh mint sprigs and extra raspberries to decorate (optional)**

Preheat the oven to 375°F. Grease a 12-by-16-inch jelly-roll pan and line with parchment paper. Use an electric mixer to beat together the egg yolks and 1 1/2 cups of the confectioners' sugar for about 3 minutes, or until pale in color and very fluffy. Set aside.

In a clean bowl, whisk the egg whites until they form soft peaks. Slowly add the remaining confectioners' sugar and whisk for another few minutes until glossy and firm.

Sift together the cocoa and cornstarch. Fold the cocoa mixture and egg whites alternately into the yolk mixture, making sure the mixture is well blended. Spread the mixture evenly on the prepared pan, and bake in the preheated oven for about 8 minutes, or until the top springs back when pressed with a fingertip. Meanwhile, whip the cream until firm peaks form. Fold in the superfine sugar and vanilla extract and set aside. Blend together the jam and water and set aside.

Lay a clean kitchen towel on your work surface and cover with a piece of parchment paper. When the sponge cake is cooked, remove from the oven and turn out onto the parchment paper. As it is cooling, trim the edges of any crusty bits. Brush a thin layer of the diluted raspberry jam to cover the entire top surface. By now there should be hardly any heat left in the cake. Quickly cover with a generous layer of the whipped cream and sprinkle generously with the fresh raspberries.

Starting at the side farthest from you, roll up the sponge cake lengthwise, finishing with the edge of the cake underneath. Transfer to a clean baking sheet and chill for at least 1 hour to set.

To serve, cut slices at an angle and serve on individual plates, decorated, if you like, with mint and extra raspberries.

OVERLEAF:
Catch of the Day, Menu 1
Smoked Eel Pâté with Fresh Herbs (page 10)
Roast Fillet of Turbot with Potato Scales (page 11)
Chocolate Roulade with Raspberries (page 12)

# Risotto Molly Malone

MOLLY AND HER WHEELBARROW MAY NEVER HAVE MADE IT TO ITALY, BUT WE'RE SURE SHE'D APPROVE OF THIS RECIPE ANYWAY. THE TASTY JUICES THAT COME FROM THE COCKLES AND MUSSELS ARE ABSORBED INTO THE RICE, MAKING IT TASTE DELICIOUS. FEEL FREE TO USE JUST COCKLES OR MUSSELS IF YOU PREFER. ARBORIO RICE IS ONE OF THE BEST RISOTTO RICES AND IS AVAILABLE IN ALL GOOD SUPERMARKETS, OR YOU CAN USE ANY MEDIUM-GRAIN RISOTTO RICE TO ACHIEVE THE WONDERFUL CREAMY TEXTURE THAT IS ESSENTIAL FOR RISOTTO. **Serves 4**

For the cockles and mussels:

**2 1/4 pounds live cockles**

**2 1/4 pounds live mussels**

**1 cup dry white wine**

**scant 1/2 cup water**

**3 tablespoons finely chopped onion**

**1 fresh thyme sprig or 1/2 teaspoon dried thyme**

**2 fresh parsley sprigs**

For the risotto:

**6 tablespoons unsalted butter**

**1 medium onion, finely chopped**

**cockle and mussel cooking liquid**

**1 cup Arborio or other risotto rice**

**salt**

**2 tablespoons chopped fresh cilantro**

**1 tablespoon snipped fresh chives**

Wash and scrub the cockles and mussels carefully, scraping off the beards from the mussels. Rinse them in clean water and discard any mussels that are open and do not close when tapped with a knife.

Meanwhile, bring the wine, water, onion, thyme and parsley to a boil in a large pan. Add the cockles and mussels, cover and boil vigorously for 2 to 3 minutes, or until all cockles and mussels have opened. Discard any that remain closed. Drain into a colander with a bowl underneath to catch and reserve the cooking liquid. Measure the liquid and add water as needed to equal 2 cups. As soon as they are cool enough to handle, remove them from their shells.

To cook the risotto, heat a large pan over medium heat. Melt 2 tablespoons of the butter and gently cook the onion until soft and translucent. Meanwhile, put the measured cockle-mussel liquid into a pan with a pinch of salt and bring it to a boil. Reduce the heat to maintain a gentle simmer. Add the rice to the onion, stir well and cook gently for about 2 minutes. Add enough of the simmering liquid just to cover the rice and stir over medium heat until most of the liquid has been absorbed into the rice. Add another good ladle of liquid and stir until this again has been absorbed. Continue in this way for about 20 minutes, or until the rice is cooked; it should be tender yet retain a little bite in the middle of each kernel. Stir in the shelled cockles and mussels, the remaining butter and the cilantro and chives and allow to warm through. Serve immediately.

# Steamed Hake

## with Sliced Tomatoes and Tarragon

ALTHOUGH WE ARE BLESSED WITH LOTS OF GOOD-QUALITY HAKE IN IRELAND, IT ISN'T ONE OF THE MOST POPULAR FISH. THAT'S BASED MORE ON HABIT THAN MERIT BECAUSE FRESH HAKE IS SUPERB. WE PARTICULARLY LIKE IT FOR THIS RECIPE BECAUSE IT LOOKS SO GOOD WITH ITS BRIGHT SILVER SKIN CONTRASTING WITH THE PURE WHITE FLESH AND THE RUBY RED TOMATOES. IF YOU CANNOT BUY HAKE EASILY, YOU CAN SUBSTITUTE ALMOST ANY GOOD, FRESH WHITE FISH. **Serves 4**

**4 hake fillets, skin on, about 6 ounces each**

**1 1/2 pounds ripe tomatoes, peeled and sliced**

For the dressing:

**1/2 teaspoon salt**

**1/4 cup lemon juice**

**2 shallots, finely chopped**

**2/3 cup extra-virgin olive oil**

**2 tablespoons chopped fresh tarragon**

To check the hake fillets for the small bones, run your fingers lightly over the flesh to locate the bones and remove them with a pair of tweezers or small pliers. Remove any scales on the skin by scraping them off with the blunt side of a knife.

Lightly oil a steamer basket or heatproof plate and set the hake fillets into it. Steam in the steamer, or cover the plate and place over a pan of boiling water, for about 6 to 8 minutes, or until tender, depending on the thickness of the fillets.

To make the dressing, dissolve the salt in the lemon juice in a small bowl. Stir in the remaining ingredients.

To serve, arrange the sliced tomatoes in a neat circle in the center of individual warmed plates. Pour a little of the dressing over and around the tomatoes. Set the hake on top of the tomatoes and serve at once.

# Roast Bananas with Waffles

BANANAS ARE A WONDERFULLY VERSATILE FRUIT THAT CAN BE USED ENDLESSLY IN DESSERTS. THEY MARRY PERFECTLY WITH CARAMEL AND RUM, AND ARE AVAILABLE ALL YEAR ROUND! A DRIZZLE OF CHOCOLATE SAUCE OR A SCOOP OF VANILLA ICE CREAM WOULD NOT GO AMISS WITH THIS DELICIOUS DESSERT. **Serves 4** (V)

For the waffles:

**3/4 cup milk**

**1/4 cup unsalted butter**

**1 cup all-purpose flour**

**4 eggs**

**1/2 cup crème fraîche or whipping cream**

**grated zest of 1/2 lemon**

**3/4 cup sugar**

**1/2 cup water**

**1/4 cup Jamaican rum**

**2 vanilla beans, split in half**

**4 ripe bananas**

Preheat the oven to 375°F.

To make the waffles, grease a waffle iron and preheat to medium-high. If you do not have a waffle iron, you can use a griddle or heavy-based frying pan.

Put the milk and butter in a pan and bring to a boil. As soon as it reaches the boiling point, remove from the heat and add all the flour at once, stirring with a wooden spoon. Place over medium heat and stir continuously for 1 to 2 minutes until it has formed a smooth mass that will not stick to the sides of the pan.

Remove from the heat and slowly beat in the eggs one at a time, either by hand or in a mixer with a dough hook. Make sure you incorporate 1 egg fully before adding the next. Lastly, pour in the crème fraîche or cream and the lemon zest and beat until well mixed.

Cook the waffles in the waffle iron following the manufacturer's instructions or on the griddle or frying pan. If working on a griddle or frying pan, cook for about 2 to 3 minutes on each side until golden.

As they are cooking, prepare the roast bananas. First make a caramel with the sugar. Place the sugar in a heavy-based pan with half the water and let it cook over high heat until it turns a nice golden caramel color. Remove from the heat immediately and add the rest of the water to stop the cooking. Add the rum and vanilla beans and leave to infuse off the heat.

Peel and cut the bananas on the diagonal into 1/2-inch slices. Place in an ovenproof dish and pour over the caramel mixture. Cover with foil and bake in the preheated oven for about 3 minutes, or until cooked through.

To serve, arrange a waffle or two (depending on size) in the center of each warmed plate. Carefully spoon the bananas over with lots of the caramel juices. Serve at once.

CHAPTER TWO

# Seafood Buffet

A buffet is a wonderful way to entertain your friends, and seafood is a great theme because it can include such a variety of recipes. They can be simple dishes for those who like the basic flavors of their food to shine through, intricate delicacies for the adventurous or traditional favorites that everyone will enjoy. Think color, texture, contrast and harmony to impress your guests.

## Menu 1

Smoked Salmon Salad Extravaganza

Lobster, Mussel and White Bean Salad

Snow Eggs in Custard with Black Currant Sauce

## Menu 2

Freshly Pickled Cod with a Parsley Aïoli

Orzo Pasta Salad with Tomatoes and Mushrooms

Creamy Leek and Shrimp Tart

Lime Tart with Papaya Sauce

## Smoked Salmon Salad Extravaganza

This is a carefully composed salad that is a feast to behold. All the ingredients have been put together to complement one another both for taste and visually. Feel free to substitute any ingredients but think about how this will affect the whole dish. **Serves 6**

**12 ounces smoked salmon slices**

**8 ounces arugula leaves**

**4 ripe tomatoes, peeled and sliced**

**1 medium cucumber**

**1 small red onion, thinly sliced**

**4 eggs, hard-boiled**

**1 tablespoon snipped fresh chives**

**1 tablespoon chive flowers**

**12 nasturtium flowers**

**fresh chervil and dill sprigs to garnish (optional)**

**Creamy Dill Dressing (see page 179) to serve**

Cut away any excess dark flesh from the salmon using a small sharp knife. Arrange the smoked salmon along the middle of a large oval platter, rolling and folding it into attractive curves. Arrange the arugula leaves all around the edges of the platter. Next lay the tomato slices on both sides of the salmon but sitting on the stems of the arugula leaves to keep them in place.

Peel the cucumber, cut it in half lengthwise and scoop out the seeds with a teaspoon. Cut each half into thin slices. Lay the cucumber inside the tomato slices next to the smoked salmon. Sprinkle the onion slices over the tomatoes and cucumber. Roughly chop the egg yolks and whites separately. Sprinkle the yolks over the arugula and the whites over the smoked salmon. Sprinkle the chives and chive flowers over the salmon. Finally scatter the nasturtium flowers and remaining herbs where you feel they look best. To serve, sprinkle generously with Creamy Dill Dressing.

## Lobster, Mussel and White Bean Salad

This is an unusual salad inspired by fresh local ingredients and a few Italian groceries. Although it's essentially a summer dish, it tastes great in the colder months, too. Adapt the recipe to whatever is available—shrimp and monkfish, or cockles and squid taste wonderful. Fresh, live lobster has the best flavor, but if you must use cooked lobster, make sure you buy it fresh from a quality supplier and omit the first cooking stage. If you are short of time, canned Italian beans work very well for this recipe. **Serves 6**

To cook the lobster, bring a large pan of water to a vigorous boil. Put in the lobster, cover and let it cook for about 18 minutes. Remove the lobster from the pan and stop the cooking process by plunging the lobster into a sink of cold water.

Insert a large knife into the lobster at the point where the tail and body are joined and cut toward the tail. The tail meat will now easily pull away from the shell. Break off the arms and claws and crack the shells with a heavy knife. Remove the meat, being careful to discard any pieces of shell. Slice the meat neatly and set aside.

To cook the mussels, simmer the wine, water, onion, thyme and parsley in a large pan. Meanwhile scrub the mussels and pull off the hairy beard with a sharp knife, then rinse them in cold water. Discard any that remain open and do not close when tapped with a knife. Add the mussels to the pan, cover and boil vigorously for 2 minutes or until all the mussels have opened. Discard any that remain closed. Drain the mussels into a colander with a bowl underneath to catch and reserve the broth. As soon as they are cool enough to handle, remove them from their shells.

To cook the soaked beans, drain and rinse them, then place them in a heavy-based pan and just cover with fresh water. Bring to a boil, then add the onion, carrot and salt. Cover and simmer gently for about 1 hour, or until the beans are tender but still hold their shape. Drain thoroughly. Toss the beans in a bowl with the lemon juice, olive oil and black pepper.

To assemble the salad, boil the mussel liquor and pour it over the beans. Add the mussels, lobster, parsley and tomatoes and toss gently. Check and adjust the seasoning to taste and serve on a large platter.

**1 lobster, 2 1/4 pounds**

For the mussels:

**1 cup dry white wine**

**7 tablespoons water**

**3 tablespoons finely chopped onion**

**1 fresh thyme sprig or 1/2 teaspoon dried thyme**

**2 fresh parsley sprigs**

**4 1/2 pounds live mussels**

For the beans:

**1 1/8 cups dried white haricot beans, soaked overnight in cold water**

**1 small onion, halved**

**1 small carrot**

**1 teaspoon salt**

**2 tablespoons lemon juice**

**6 tablespoons olive oil**

**1/2 teaspoon cracked black pepper**

To garnish:

**2 cups fresh flat-leaf parsley leaves**

**4 large plum tomatoes, peeled and roughly chopped**

**salt**

# Snow Eggs in Custard
## with Black Currant Sauce

THESE GENTLY POACHED MERINGUE EGGS ARE LIGHT AS A FEATHER, THE PERFECT WAY TO END A MEAL. THE CUSTARD SAUCE COULD BE FLAVORED WITH LAVENDER ESSENCE RATHER THAN VANILLA FOR AN ESPECIALLY LAVISH TOUCH. FROZEN BLACK CURRANTS ARE FINE FOR THIS DISH; LEAVE THEM TO THAW NATURALLY BEFORE USING. ANY BERRIES OR MIXTURE OF BERRIES SUCH AS RASPBERRIES OR BLUEBERRIES COULD BE SUBSTITUTED. REDUCE SUGAR TO TASTE. **Serves 6 to 8** (V)

For the custard:

**4 1/4 cups milk**

**1 vanilla bean, split lengthwise, or 1 tablespoon vanilla extract**

**12 egg yolks, beaten**

**1 1/4 cups superfine sugar**

For the snow eggs:

**5 cups water**

**6 egg whites**

**1 cup superfine sugar**

For the black currant sauce:

**9 ounces black currants**

**5 tablespoons water**

**2/3 cup superfine sugar**

**1 to 2 teaspoons lemon juice**

**about 2 tablespoons sliced almonds to garnish**

To make the custard sauce, place the milk and split vanilla bean (if using extract, you will add it later) in a heavy-based pan. Bring to a boil, then remove from the heat and allow to infuse for at least 30 minutes. In a medium-sized bowl, whisk together the egg yolks and sugar until the sugar has dissolved. Slowly pour in the boiled milk, whisking continuously. Pour the whole mixture back into a clean pan and stir over medium heat for about 5 to 10 minutes, or until thick. Do not allow the custard to boil. You can test that the custard is cooked by holding the spoon up and drawing a line through the custard on the spoon with your finger. If the line holds, it is ready. Place a fine sieve over a clean serving container and strain the custard into it. Allow to cool. (If using vanilla extract, rather than the bean, add at this point.)

To make the snow eggs, in a large, low-sided pan or nonstick frying pan, bring the water to a simmer. Meanwhile, whisk the egg whites until they form soft peaks. Slowly add the sugar, beating gently, then whisk vigorously for 1 minute until the whites are firm and glossy.

Place a large dampened piece of parchment paper flat on your work surface. Fill a pastry bag fitted with a large star nozzle with the meringue mixture and pipe about 12 portions, each about 3 inches in diameter and about 2 inches high onto the dampened parchment paper. Carefully lift each one with a spatula and flip upside down into the simmering water. Only place as many in the pan as will fit comfortably; you don't really want them to touch one another while poaching. Poach, without allowing the water to boil, for 5 minutes.

Use a slotted spoon to turn each of them over gently, then poach for a further 3 minutes until firm.

Carefully lift out the meringues and place on a clean kitchen towel to drain. Cook the remaining meringues in the same way. Place the drained cooked snow eggs on the custard and chill in the fridge for at least 1 hour. Don't crowd the eggs as they are fragile.

While the custard and eggs are chilling, make the black currant sauce. Simply place all the ingredients in a blender or food processor and process. Pass though a fine sieve and taste for flavor. Adjust with more sugar or lemon juice as necessary. Set aside.

Toast the sliced almonds by placing under a medium-hot broiler or in a 350°F oven until golden.

To serve, bring the serving dish out of the refrigerator and sprinkle on the sliced almonds, or carefully arrange a couple of snow eggs in the center of individual soup plates and ladle some of the custard sauce around them. Decorate with toasted almonds and serve the black currant sauce separately.

# Freshly Pickled Cod
## with a Parsley Aïoli

POACHED FISH SERVED WITH A MINIMUM OF FUSS IS PURE AND DELICIOUS. HERE THE COD IS POACHED AND ALLOWED TO COOL IN AN AROMATIC BROTH CALLED A COURT BOUILLON. IT CAN BE SERVED STRAIGHTAWAY OR IT CAN BE CHILLED FOR A DAY OR TWO, THEN ALLOWED TO RETURN TO ROOM TEMPERATURE BEFORE SERVING. ADD AS MUCH OR AS LITTLE GARLIC TO THE AÏOLI AS YOU PREFER. **Serves 6**

**6 cod steaks, about 3 1/2 ounces each**

For the court bouillon:

**1/4 cup white wine vinegar**

**1 cup dry white wine**

**2 cups water**

**1 small carrot, neatly sliced**

**1 small onion, neatly sliced**

**1 garlic clove, sliced**

**1 bay leaf**

**1/2 teaspoon coriander seeds**

**1/4 teaspoon fennel seeds**

**6 white peppercorns**

**1 tablespoon salt**

For the aïoli:

**1 bunch fresh parsley, stems removed**

**3 egg yolks**

**2 to 4 garlic cloves, finely chopped**

**1 1/2 tablespoons lemon juice**

**1/2 teaspoon salt**

**1 cup light olive oil**

**1 cup vegetable oil**

Put all the ingredients for the court bouillon in a large pan. Bring to a boil over medium heat and simmer gently for 15 to 20 minutes, or until the carrots are tender. Remove from the heat and allow to infuse for at least 1 hour.

To cook the cod, return the court bouillon to a boil. Add the cod steaks and simmer over very low heat for about 2 minutes. Remove the pan from the heat and allow the cod to finish cooking as it cools down.

To make the aïoli, bring a pan of water to a boil, add the parsley leaves and blanch for 30 seconds, then drain and refresh under cold water. Pat dry with kitchen paper and chop roughly.

In a blender or food processor, combine the parsley, egg yolks, garlic, lemon juice and salt. Blend for a few seconds, then slowly add the oils in a steady stream until emulsified. Set aside.

To serve, place the cod steaks on a large serving platter with the vegetables and a little of the court bouillon. Serve the aïoli on the side.

# Orzo Pasta Salad
## with Tomatoes and Mushrooms

ORZO IS A PASTA SHAPE THAT IS JUST A LITTLE LARGER THAN LONG-GRAIN RICE. IT IS NORMALLY USED IN ITALIAN SOUPS LIKE MINESTRONE, BUT IT WORKS VERY WELL FOR PASTA SALADS. IF YOU CAN'T FIND ORZO, SUBSTITUTE YOUR FAVORITE PASTA SHAPE. **Serves 6** (V)

**8 ounces orzo pasta**

**10 ounces mushrooms, sliced or quartered**

**6 tablespoons finely chopped onion**

**3 tablespoons lemon juice**

**1/2 teaspoon salt**

**3 tablespoons olive oil**

**3 ripe tomatoes, peeled, seeded and diced**

**2 tablespoons chopped fresh parsley**

**1 tablespoon chopped fresh dill (optional)**

**salt and fresh ground black pepper**

Bring 3 quarts of salted water to a boil in a large pan. Add the orzo, stir well, then return the water to a boil. Cook until just al dente. Drain the pasta and refresh under cold running water. Allow to drain well in a colander while you prepare the mushrooms.

Bring 7 tablespoons of water to a boil in a pan. Add the mushrooms, onion, lemon juice and salt. Cover and cook for 4 minutes. Allow to cool slightly, then add all the remaining ingredients.

Combine the orzo with the mushroom mixture in an attractive serving bowl. Check the seasoning and adjust to taste with salt and pepper.

OVERLEAF:

Seafood Buffet, Menu 2

Freshly Pickled Cod with a Parsley Aïoli (page 24)

Orzo Pasta Salad with Tomatoes and Mushrooms (page 25)

Creamy Leek and Shrimp Tart (page 28)

Lime Tart with Papaya Sauce (page 29)

# Creamy Leek and Shrimp Tart

Remember when quiche was the latest trendy food? Nowadays it has gone out of fashion, so when we have it on the menu at the restaurant we call it a tart. People love it and we invariably run out, which is encouraging because a great dish should not be forsaken just because of fickle fashion. The tart tastes superb served just warm with a small salad.

**Serves 6**

**8 ounces Savory Pastry (see page 177)**

For the filling:

**2 tablespoons unsalted butter**

**7 tablespoons water**

**1/2 teaspoon salt**

**7 ounces leeks, thinly sliced**

**7 ounces cooked peeled shrimp or prawns**

**3 eggs**

**3 egg yolks**

**1 1/2 cups whipping cream**

**3 tablespoons tomato ketchup**

**1 tablespoon chopped fresh herbs such as parsley, tarragon, chives, basil**

**1/2 teaspoon salt**

**pinch of white pepper**

Preheat the oven to 350°F. Grease an 8-inch tart pan with a removable bottom.

Roll out the pastry and use it to line the prepared pan. Place in the refrigerator to chill for at least 20 minutes.

Cover the pastry with foil and fill with pie weights. Bake blind in the preheated oven for about 10 minutes, or until light golden brown. Remove the weights and foil and set the pastry shell aside to cool.

Reduce the oven temperature to 300°F.

To cook the leeks, melt the butter in a pan with the water and salt. Add the leeks and fry gently for about 4 to 5 minutes, or until just cooked. Allow the leeks to cool slightly, then squeeze out all the excess liquid. Pat the shrimp dry on paper towels and mix them with the leeks.

In a medium bowl, whisk together the eggs and egg yolks until well blended. Add the remaining ingredients and whisk gently until the mixture is smooth. Stir in the shrimp-leek mixture. Gently pour the filling into the pastry shell and cook in the preheated oven for about 40 minutes, or until the tart is completely set. Allow to cool slightly before serving.

# Lime Tart with Papaya Sauce

PAPAYA AND LIME MAY NOT BE THE FIRST INGREDIENTS YOU THINK OF IN RELATION TO IRISH COOKING, BUT THEY ARE A MATCH MADE IN HEAVEN! OFTEN WE SERVE THIS TART WITH A PAPAYA SORBET. IF YOU HAVE AN ICE CREAM MACHINE, YOU COULD TURN THE PAPAYA SAUCE INTO A SORBET WITH PERFECT RESULTS. IF PREFERRED, THIS TART COULD BE PAIRED WITH MANGO OR BLACKBERRIES. **Serves 6 to 8** (V)

For the lime tart:

**8 ounces Shortcrust Pastry (see page 177)**

**8 eggs**

**1 2/3 cups superfine sugar**

**grated zest of 4 limes**

**1 cup whipping cream**

**juice of 10 to 12 limes**

**1 egg yolk, lightly beaten**

For the papaya sauce:

**2 ripe papayas**

**juice of 3 to 4 limes**

**6 tablespoons granulated sugar**

**7 tablespoons water**

Preheat the oven to 375°F. Grease a 9-inch tart pan with a removable bottom.

Roll out the pastry about 1/8 inch thick and use it to line the prepared pan. Place in the refrigerator to chill for 30 minutes.

Whisk the eggs, sugar and lime zest until light in color and the mixture trails off the whisk in ribbons. Slowly whisk in the cream. Slowly add three-quarters of the lime juice. Taste the mixture and add as much of the remaining juice as you like. Set aside.

Cover the pastry with foil and fill with pie weights. Bake blind in the preheated oven for about 10 to 15 minutes. Remove the weights and foil and return the pastry to the oven for another 1 to 2 minutes. Remove from the oven and brush the base and sides with the egg yolk to seal the pastry. Leave to cool slightly.

Reduce the oven temperature to 325°F. Fill the pastry shell with the lime mixture to just below the rim of the pastry. Bake in the preheated oven for about 25 to 30 minutes. This slower cooking ensures a smooth texture, just as one would cook a caramel custard slowly. When only the very center jiggles slightly, the tart is cooked. Remove from the oven and leave to cool.

To make the papaya sauce, halve the papayas and discard the seeds. Scoop out the flesh and place in a blender or food processor with the lime juice, sugar and water. Purée, then pass through a fine sieve. Taste to check the flavor and reduce tartness by adding a little more sugar, or sweetness by adding a little more lime juice.

To serve, place a wedge of lime tart on individual plates and ladle the papaya sauce around. Serve at once.

CHAPTER THREE

# Summer Barbecue

Most people get excited about the prospect of a barbecue and with very good reason: the possibilities are endless. Don't just stick to the old standbys, think of the colors and flavors of Mediterranean and ethnic foods, and use herbs and spices to infuse your dishes with zest and aroma.

### Menu 1

Salmon Wrapped in Zucchini Ribbons with Tomato Vinaigrette

Summer Barbecue Mixed Grill

Romaine Salad Boats

Lemon Cake with Nectarines and Blackberries

### Menu 2

Eggplant and Olive Bruschetta

Shrimp Kebabs with Sun-Dried Tomato Vinaigrette

Rice Salad with Grilled Red Onions, Peppers and Cilantro

Almond Meringue and Apricot Cream Sandwich

# Salmon Wrapped in Zucchini Ribbons
## with Tomato Vinaigrette

SALMON IS FANTASTIC FOR A SUMMER BARBECUE. ITS NATURAL OILS PROTECT IT FROM THE HARSH HEAT OF THE FLAMES. HOWEVER, NO AMOUNT OF OIL WILL PROTECT YOUR SALMON IF YOU OVERCOOK IT, SO BE DARING AND TRY IT A LITTLE UNDERDONE. SOAKING WOODEN SKEWERS BEFOREHAND WILL PREVENT THEM FROM CHARRING WHILE ON THE BARBECUE. **Serves 6**

**1 1/2 pounds fresh salmon, skinned and boned**

**3 medium zucchini**

**salt and freshly ground black pepper**

**2 tablespoons light olive oil**

For the vinaigrette:

**4 plum tomatoes, peeled, seeded and diced**

**2 cups fresh basil leaves, chopped**

**7 tablespoons extra-virgin olive oil**

**1 tablespoon lemon juice**

**1/4 teaspoon salt**

**1/4 teaspoon cracked black pepper**

Soak six 6-inch wooden skewers in water for at least 30 minutes. (You may use any length wooden skewer you have.) Preheat the barbecue or broiler.

Cut the salmon fillet into 1-inch dice or into 24 even pieces. With a potato peeler, peel 5-inch ribbons off the zucchini. Carefully wrap each cube of salmon with a strip of zucchini. Slice and skewer each piece as it is prepared, allowing about 4 pieces of salmon per skewer. Season each one with a little salt and pepper, brush with a little olive oil and cook on the barbecue or in the broiler for about 5 minutes, turning occasionally, until firm and cooked.

While the salmon is cooking, mix all the ingredients for the vinaigrette in a small bowl, then divide among warmed plates. When the salmon is ready, lift the brochettes onto the plates and serve immediately.

# Summer Barbecue Mixed Grill

If you are using the barbecue, you may as well cook a few different things—especially since you won't have any extra pans to clean. Here we have three meats, so work ahead and marinate the chicken and lamb the day before; they'll be all the better for it. The sausages can be blanched beforehand, too, so that they only need to be browned and heated in order to serve. And the potatoes? Well, of course, in Ireland we barbecue them as well! As an alternative to the Romaine Salad Boats (see page 34), the Salad of Herbs (see page 169) also makes a delicious accompaniment. **Serves 6**

**6 to 12 thick pork sausages**

For the lamb:

**1 1/2 pounds boneless lamb from leg**

**7 tablespoons light olive oil**

**1 tablespoon chopped fresh rosemary**

**2 garlic cloves, crushed**

**1 bay leaf**

For the chicken:

**4 tablespoons vegetable oil**

**2 teaspoons curry powder**

**2 tablespoons dark soy sauce**

**1 1/2 pounds boneless, skinless chicken thighs or breasts**

Soak six 6-inch wooden skewers in water for at least 30 minutes. (You may use any length wooden skewer you have.) Preheat the barbecue or broiler.

To blanch the sausages, bring a large pan of water to a boil. Add the sausages, return to a boil, then simmer for 1 minute. Drain and refresh in cold water, then chill until needed.

For the lamb, trim off any excess fat and cut into 1-inch dice. Thread on to the skewers and lay in a porcelain or stainless steel dish. Simply cover with the rosemary, garlic and bay leaf and chill for at least 12 hours.

For the chicken, mix together the vegetable oil, curry powder and soy sauce in a porcelain or stainless steel dish. Add the chicken and rub the marinade into it. Cover and chill for at least 6 hours.

Cut the potatoes in half lengthwise and toss with all the remaining ingredients in a large bowl. Season with salt and place them cut-side down on the barbecue. When the potatoes are well marked and nicely brown, turn them skin-side down and cook for a further 2 minutes. Place them in the oven to keep warm while you barbecue the meat.

Remove the lamb kebabs from the marinade and season with salt and pepper. Place on the barbecue and grill for about 4 minutes for medium-rare or 8 minutes for well done. Remove the chicken from the marinade and season with salt and pepper. Grill on the barbecue for about 6 to 8 minutes, or until firm. Brown the sausages quickly on the edges of the barbecue while the other meats are finishing. Serve at once.

For the potatoes:

**2 1/2 pounds small waxy potatoes, cooked**

**1/2 teaspoon dried oregano**

**1/2 teaspoon dried thyme**

**1 teaspoon ground red chili**

**4 tablespoons oil**

**salt and freshly ground black pepper**

# Romaine Salad Boats

THIS IS A FUN LITTLE SALAD THAT CAN BE BUILT WITH WHATEVER IS ON HAND. **Serves 6** 

**12 romaine salad leaves, preferably from the heart**

**2 avocados, peeled and diced**

**4 plum tomatoes, diced**

**1 1/2 ounces alfalfa sprouts**

**3 eggs, hard-boiled and roughly chopped**

For the dressing:

**6 tablespoons mayonnaise**

**3 tablespoons water**

**1 teaspoon Dijon mustard**

**1 teaspoon chopped fresh dill (optional)**

**salt and freshly ground black pepper**

Arrange the salad leaves on a large platter with the edges facing up so that they look like boats. Combine the avocados, tomatoes and sprouts in a bowl, then fill each of the salad leaves with this mixture. Sprinkle each one with some chopped egg.

Whisk all the dressing ingredients together in a small bowl. Check and adjust the seasoning to taste, then spoon over the salad and serve at once.

# Lemon Cake
## with Nectarines and Blackberries

A LIGHT, TANGY CAKE LIKE THIS ONE REVIVES THE TASTE BUDS AFTER A SUBSTANTIAL MEAL. SELECT THE BEST-QUALITY FRUIT IN SEASON, OR SERVE THE CAKE ON ITS OWN OR WITH SOME WHIPPED CREAM. THE CAKE KEEPS VERY WELL WHEN COMPLETELY WRAPPED IN PLASTIC WRAP; WE FEEL IT'S EVEN TASTIER THE NEXT DAY.

**Serves 8 to 10** 

**4 eggs, separated**

**1 1/4 cups superfine sugar**

**3/4 cup buttermilk**

**6 tablespoons lemon juice**

**grated zest of 2 lemons**

**1 3/4 cups all-purpose flour**

**1 1/4 teaspoons baking powder**

**1/4 teaspoon salt**

**1/2 cup plus 1 tablespoon unsalted butter, melted and cooled**

For the glaze:

**6 tablespoons lemon juice**

**1 1/2 cups confectioners' sugar, sifted**

For fruit decoration:

**3 or 4 ripe nectarines, thinly sliced**

**1 pint (2 cups) fresh blackberries, hulled**

Preheat the oven to 350°F. Grease a 9-inch spring form pan, then line the bottom with parchment paper.

Whisk together the egg yolks and 2/3 cup of the sugar for 3 minutes. Slowly add the buttermilk, whisking gently, followed by the lemon juice and zest. Set aside.

In a clean bowl, whisk the egg whites until they form soft peaks. Whisking gently, pour in the remaining sugar in a slow, steady stream. Whisk vigorously for 1 minute until the whites are glossy and firm.

Sift together the flour, baking powder and salt. Gently fold spoonfuls of the flour mixture, then the egg whites into the egg yolk mixture until all the ingredients are well blended. Take a big serving spoon of this mixture, stir it into the cooled melted butter and mix well. Fold this butter mixture into the main bowl until everything is well mixed together. Pour into the prepared pan and cook in the preheated oven for 1 hour, or until a skewer inserted into the middle comes out clean. Remove from the oven and let the cake cool for 10 minutes, then turn out onto a wire rack to finish cooling. Using a sharp knife or skewer, poke the cake many times all over. The little holes will help the cake absorb the glaze.

To make the glaze, bring the lemon juice and confectioners' sugar to a boil in a small pan. Boil gently for a few minutes until it thickens and has a saucelike consistency. Gently ladle the glaze over the cake, giving the cake time to absorb the glaze so that it does not all run off the sides. Dust the cake with a little more confectioners' sugar and then slice it. Serve each slice on a plate and decorate with a few slices of the nectarines and a handful of berries.

# Eggplant and Olive Bruschetta

BRUSCHETTA ARE GREAT FUN. IN THEIR PUREST FORM, THEY ARE SLICES OF COUNTRY BREAD TOASTED OVER OPEN COALS, THEN RUBBED WITH GARLIC WHILE STILL WARM AND DRIZZLED WITH PURE GREEN OLIVE OIL. THIS IS A SIMPLE RECIPE THAT WE'RE PARTICULARLY FOND OF, SO WHEN WE LIGHT THE BARBECUE WE ALWAYS MAKE BRUSCHETTA. TAPENADE IS A DELICIOUS OLIVE PASTE THAT IS NOW WIDELY AVAILABLE IN SUPERMARKETS. **Serves 6** (V)

**2 large eggplants, sliced 3/4 inch thick**

**6 large slices hearty country bread, each 1 inch thick**

**2/3 cup olive oil**

**salt and freshly ground black pepper**

**2 garlic cloves, peeled**

**6 tablespoons tapenade**

Preheat the barbecue.

With a pastry brush, brush the slices of eggplant and the bread lightly with olive oil on both sides. When the barbecue is ready, season the eggplant slices with salt and pepper and grill for 3 to 5 minutes on each side, or until they are beautifully brown and soft right through. When the eggplants are nearly cooked, start to grill the bread slices. Don't put the bread on the hottest part of the grill or the slices will burn before they are properly toasted. Grill the bread until it is crisp and nicely brown. When the bread is cooked, rub it twice with a garlic clove, then spread it with a tablespoon of tapenade. Finish with a few slices of grilled eggplant and serve while still warm.

# Shrimp Kebabs
## with Sun-Dried Tomato Vinaigrette

Paul read the other day in a top magazine that sun-dried tomatoes were out of fashion. The poor old sun-dried tomato—it's hardly in and it's out again. What a load of rubbish! We believe that if you enjoy something—a recipe or an ingredient—you should stick by it. This sun-dried tomato vinaigrette is also fabulous with salmon. **Serves 6**

**36 large shrimp, peeled and deveined (2 pounds)**

**12 green onions, trimmed**

**1/4 teaspoon freshly ground black pepper**

**1/2 teaspoon salt**

**1 tablespoon chopped fresh parsley**

**1 tablespoon olive oil**

**a few salad leaves and parsley sprigs to garnish**

For the vinaigrette:

**12 sun-dried tomatoes in oil, about 4 ounces, roughly chopped**

**3/4 cup plus 2 tablespoons light olive oil**

**1 teaspoon lemon juice**

**1/2 teaspoon ground red chili (optional)**

Soak six wooden skewers in water for at least 30 minutes. Preheat the barbecue or broiler.

To make the vinaigrette, blend together all the ingredients in a food processor for about 1 minute, or until the vinaigrette has a fairly smooth texture. Taste for seasoning because sun-dried tomatoes vary greatly in the amount of salt and flavor they contain. Adjust the seasoning to taste.

In a large bowl, toss the shrimp and green onions with the seasonings, parsley and oil. Thread the shrimp and onions onto the skewers, starting with an onion followed by 6 shrimp, then finishing with an onion. Grill on the barbecue for 2 minutes on each side. Serve on warmed plates with a generous spoonful of sun-dried tomato vinaigrette and a few nice salad leaves and parsley sprigs.

OVERLEAF:
Summer Barbecue, Menu 2
Eggplant and Olive Bruschetta (page 36)
Shrimp Kebabs with Sun-Dried Tomato Vinaigrette (page 37)
Rice Salad with Grilled Red Onions, Peppers and Cilantro (page 40)
Almond Meringue and Apricot Cream Sandwich (page 41)

# Rice Salad
## with Grilled Red Onions, Peppers and Cilantro

RICE SALADS ARE GREAT IN CONCEPT BUT THEY CAN BE TERRIBLY DISAPPOINTING. THIS ONE, HOWEVER, IS PACKED FULL OF FLAVOR SINCE THE PEPPERS AND ONIONS ARE FIRST GRILLED ON THE BARBECUE AND THEN CHOPPED AND THROWN IN AT THE LAST MINUTE. IF YOU NEED TO GET EVERYTHING READY WELL IN ADVANCE, SIMPLY DICE THE PEPPERS AND ONIONS AND SAUTÉ THEM IN A LITTLE OLIVE OIL INSTEAD. **Serves 6** 

**1 2/3 cups long-grain rice**

**6 tablespoons Standard Vinaigrette (see page 178)**

**2 large red chilies, seeded and finely chopped**

**3 tablespoons chopped fresh cilantro**

**1 red onion**

**salt and freshly ground black pepper**

**1 tablespoon olive oil**

**1 small yellow bell pepper**

**1 small red bell pepper**

Preheat the barbecue.

Cook the rice in plenty of boiling salted water, following the directions on the packet, until just tender. Drain and refresh under cold water. Pat the rice dry in a clean cloth, then place in a serving bowl. Stir in the vinaigrette, chilies and cilantro. Check and adjust the seasoning to taste.

Slice the red onion into 4 or 5 thick slices, season with a little salt and pepper and rub with olive oil. Rub the peppers with a little olive oil. When the barbecue is lit but not quite ready, put the peppers on the grill until the skins are quite charred. Now add the onions and grill for about 2 minutes on each side. Remove when they are cool enough to handle. Peel and seed the peppers and cut them into fine dice. Then dice the red onions. Add them to the rice salad and serve immediately.

# Almond Meringue and Apricot Cream Sandwich

THIS MOIST NUT MERINGUE IS A DELICIOUS FOOLPROOF RECIPE THAT COULD BE PUT WITH ANY FRUIT TO CREATE A STUNNING DESSERT. YOU COULD SUBSTITUTE GROUND HAZELNUTS, PECANS OR WALNUTS FOR THE ALMONDS, BUT BE SURE TO SKIN THEM FIRST OR THE RESULTING MERINGUE WILL BE BITTER. YOU CAN OF COURSE USE FRESH APRICOTS IF YOU JUST LIGHTLY POACH THEM. **Serves 6** (V)

For the meringue:

**6 egg whites**

**1 cup less 1 tablespoon superfine sugar**

**scant 2 cups ground almonds**

For the apricot cream:

**1 1/4 cups dried apricots**

**1 1/2 cups water**

**3/4 cup superfine sugar**

**1 1/2 tablespoons lemon juice**

**1 cup whipping cream, softly whipped**

**1 can or jar (12 ounces) apricots, drained and cut into 1/2-inch dice**

**confectioners' sugar for dusting**

Preheat the oven to 350°F. Line a 12-inch square baking sheet with aluminum foil.

Whisk the egg whites gently for 30 seconds, then whisk more vigorously for 1 minute, or until they hold soft peaks. Add 1/4 cup of the sugar in a slow, steady stream, whisking vigorously until the whites are thick and glossy.

Sift the remaining sugar with the ground almonds, sprinkle the mixture over the egg whites and fold in gently until just combined. Spread the meringue in an even layer over the prepared baking sheet so that it covers the whole sheet and is even in thickness. Bake in the preheated oven for about 30 minutes, or until light golden brown and crisp but not dried out. The result should be a chewy, moist meringue, not a dry crumbly one. Remove from the oven and lift carefully onto a wire rack to cool.

Place the dried apricots, water, sugar and lemon juice in a pan and bring to a simmer over medium heat. Simmer gently for about 1 hour, or until the apricots are very soft. Remove from the heat and leave to cool slightly. Purée in a blender or food processor, then pass through a fine sieve. The resulting purée should be quite thick and intense in flavor. Fold this purée into the softly whipped cream and reserve in the refrigerator.

To assemble the dessert, cut 12 equal-sized rectangles from the meringue and arrange half of them on 6 individual plates. Top with a generous spoonful of apricot cream and sprinkle generously with diced apricot. Dust the remaining meringue rectangles with a little confectioners' sugar, then place on top of the apricots. Serve at once.

CHAPTER FOUR

# Winter Cravings

The short days of winter, the bleak nights and the rain that never seems to end conjure up visions of huddling round a blazing fire yearning for comforting food that offers warmth as well as consolation. These winter recipes fit the bill perfectly.

Menu 1

Warm Potato and Blood Sausage Salad

Roast Goose with Traditional Sage and Onion Stuffing

Tangy Beet Purée

Warm Apple Charlotte

Menu 2

Smoked Salmon with Scrambled Eggs

Braised Lamb Shanks
with Pearl Barley and Root Vegetables

Christmas Pudding Parfait

# Warm Potato and Blood Sausage Salad

THIS IS A SIMPLE MEAT AND TWO VEG SALAD THAT CAN BE SERVED AS A TASTY STARTER OR A SATISFYING LUNCH DISH. FEEL FREE TO SUBSTITUTE OTHER SAUSAGES FOR THE BLOOD SAUSAGES IF YOU PREFER, BUT THE VERSION THAT WE GIVE HERE DOES HAVE MORE DRAMATIC COLOR! **Serves 6**

**12 small waxy salad potatoes**

**3/4 cup Standard Vinaigrette (see page 178)**

**2 shallots, finely diced**

**1 tablespoon chopped fresh parsley**

**salt and freshly ground black pepper**

**1 1/2 tablespoons vegetable oil**

**1 pound blood sausages, cut into 1/2-inch-thick slices**

**12 ounces broccoli florets**

**5 tablespoons meat gravy (optional)**

**1 1/2 tablespoons snipped fresh chives (optional)**

Place the potatoes in a small pan, cover with lightly salted water, bring to a boil and simmer over medium-high heat until tender. Drain and allow to cool slightly. Peel the potatoes and slice into 1/4-inch-thick slices. In a small bowl, toss the potatoes in the vinaigrette with the shallots and parsley. Season with a little salt and pepper.

Heat a large frying pan over medium heat, add the oil and blood sausage and cook for 3 minutes on each side. Add to the potatoes.

While the sausages are cooking, bring a large pan of lightly salted water to a boil, drop in the broccoli florets and cook for 4 minutes. Drain thoroughly and add to the potatoes.

To serve, gently toss the potatoes with the broccoli and sausage. Spoon onto warmed serving plates. Finish with a spoonful of gravy, if using, and snipped chives.

# Roast Goose
## with Traditional Sage and Onion Stuffing

THERE'S NO DOUBT THAT GOOSE IS DELICIOUS, BUT IT CAN BE DISAPPOINTING BECAUSE OF ITS LOW YIELD OF MEAT, SO ALLOW ABOUT 1 1/2 POUNDS PER PERSON. THIS RECIPE WILL GIVE YOU A DELICIOUS LIGHT GRAVY THAT REALLY SUITS THE RICHNESS OF THE GOOSE MEAT. THE TANGY BEET PURÉE (SEE PAGE 48) IS THE PERFECT ACCOMPANIMENT. **Serves 6 to 8**

**3 tablespoons unsalted butter**

**1 1/2 pounds onions, minced or finely chopped**

**salt**

**30 fresh sage leaves, chopped**

**1 goose liver, chopped (optional)**

**6 ounces bulk sausage meat**

**2 egg yolks**

**3 cups fresh bread crumbs**

**freshly ground black pepper**

**1 goose, about 11 pounds**

**2 cups chicken stock, broth or water**

**unsalted butter, chilled and diced**

Preheat the oven to 425°F.

In a large pan, melt the butter and cook the onions over low heat with a pinch of salt for 10 minutes. Add the sage leaves and the liver and cook for a further 2 minutes. Tip the onion mixture into a large bowl and allow to cool slightly. Mix in the sausage, egg yolks and bread crumbs and season generously with salt and pepper.

Season the goose lightly inside and out and insert the stuffing into the body cavity. Tie the legs together tightly and prick the skin with a toothpick or trussing needle to allow the fat to escape during cooking.

Lay the goose in a deep roasting pan and cook in the preheated oven for 30 minutes. Reduce the oven temperature to 300°F and cook for a further 2 1/2 hours, basting the goose with its own fat about every 20 minutes.

Remove the goose from the oven, place on a warmed serving platter and cover with foil to rest for about 15 minutes. Pour off the fat from the roasting pan, saving all the dark roasting juices. Deglaze the roasting pan with the chicken stock, broth, or water, scraping all the caramelized juices off the bottom of the pan. Strain the juices into a clean pan and boil until reduced to about 1 1/4 cups. Finally, whisk in the butter to achieve the desired consistency and check and adjust the seasoning to taste.

To carve the goose, remove the legs and breasts first. To do this, cut the skin where the legs meet the breasts. Turn the goose on its side. Hold the drumstick with a clean cloth and pull the entire leg down toward the back. The thigh bone should pop out of its socket so that you only have to cut any awkward tendons to release the leg. Repeat with the other leg. Cut through the legs to release the drumsticks and cut each of the thighs in half, parallel to the thigh bone. This will give you six leg portions. If you need eight, utilize the wings. To release the breasts, cut along each side of the breastbone. You can then easily push the breasts away from the bone with your knife or fingers. Set the breasts on a board and cut each into 6 or 8 pieces, depending on how many servings you require. You should now have 2 slices of breast and 1 leg serving per person.

If you wish to work ahead, it is possible to do most of this in advance and simply place the portioned goose meat skin-side up on a clean baking sheet; but don't slice the breast meat until you are ready to serve. Preheat on a low shelf underneath a hot broiler with the oven door closed for about 5 minutes.

OVERLEAF:

Winter Cravings, Menu 1

Warm Potato and Blood Sausage Salad (page 43)

Roast Goose with Traditional Sage and Onion Stuffing (page 44)

Warm Apple Charlotte (page 48)

# Tangy Beet Purée

A WONDERFUL JAZZY BEET RECIPE THAT GOES VERY WELL WITH GOOSE, DUCK, PORK OR GAME. **Serves 6** 

**12 ounces cooked beets, sliced (about 3 beets)**

**1 medium onion, finely chopped**

**1 garlic clove, crushed**

**3 tablespoons red wine vinegar**

**2 tomatoes, peeled, seeded and chopped**

**6 tablespoons stock or broth**

**1 teaspoon sugar**

**salt and freshly ground black pepper**

Preheat the oven to 350°F.

Combine all the ingredients in a baking dish and cover tightly with foil. Cook in the preheated oven for 1 hour. Remove from the oven and purée in a blender or food processor until smooth. Check and adjust the seasoning to taste. Serve immediately.

# Warm Apple Charlotte

WHAT MAKES A REALLY GREAT APPLE CHARLOTTE? QUALITY INGREDIENTS, OF COURSE, FROM GOOD BREAD AND FRESH BUTTER TO TASTY BUT TART COOKING APPLES. THIS IS ONE DESSERT THAT WILL NEVER GO OUT OF FASHION. YOU NEED TO USE METAL MOLDS OR THE BREAD WILL NOT COLOR PROPERLY. SERVE WITH VANILLA CUSTARD SAUCE (SEE PAGE 181), TOFFEE SAUCE (SEE PAGE 184) OR JUST SOME SOFTLY WHIPPED CREAM. **Serves 6**

**1 3/4 pounds cooking apples**

**1 1/2 cups unsalted butter, softened**

**3/4 cup superfine sugar**

**grated zest and juice of 1 small lemon**

**about 3/4 loaf white bread**

Preheat the oven to 400°F.

Peel and core the apples and chop them roughly. Place in a heavy-based pan with a spoonful of the butter. Add about 9 tablespoons of sugar, the lemon juice and zest and cook over medium heat until it is all soft and pulpy. Do not cover, as you want as much moisture to evaporate off as possible, leaving a more solid mass of apple purée. Don't worry if there are some chunks; a bit of texture is nice. Adjust the flavor by adding more sugar if necessary.

Using a pastry brush, generously grease six 3/4-cup metal molds with some of the softened butter. Sprinkle about 4 tablespoons of sugar into the first mold, shake it about until the whole mold is well covered with sugar. Pour the excess into the next mold and do the same until you have sugared all the molds.

Remove the crusts and slice the bread into 1/4-inch-thick slices. Using the pastry brush, generously coat both sides of each slice with the softened butter. Cut a round of bread to fit the bottom of each mold and then cut several slices into strips about 1 1/2 inches wide. Line the sides of each mold with the strips, slightly overlapping each to ensure no apple will escape through during the baking stage. These strips should ideally be about 1/4 inch higher than the sides of the mold.

Now fill each mold nearly to the top with the cooled apple purée and finish by using any leftover bread pieces to cover the top. As this will be the bottom when served, it doesn't matter too much what it looks like, as long as the purée is completely covered.

Bake the charlottes in the preheated oven for about 10 minutes. Reduce the oven temperature to 325°F and continue to cook for a further 20 to 30 minutes. The bread should be golden and firm and the charlottes should not collapse when turned out. Remove from the oven.

To serve, simply turn out the charlottes onto individual warmed plates and serve warm but not too hot with an accompanying sauce of your choice.

# Smoked Salmon
## with Scrambled Eggs

THIS DISH IS ALL ABOUT GOOD INGREDIENTS AND A LITTLE PATIENCE. THE SALMON SHOULD BE FRESH AND NOT TOO SMOKY. THE EGGS SHOULD BE FREE-RANGE WITH DEEPLY COLORED YOLKS. AND THE PATIENCE COMES IN WHEN YOU'RE COOKING THE EGGS. THEY MUST BE STIRRED OVER LOW HEAT UNTIL THEY JUST COME TOGETHER IN SOFT CURDS. AS A DELICIOUS ALTERNATIVE, USE PUFF PASTRY CASES INSTEAD OF THE TOASTED BAGUETTE SLICES. **Serves 4**

**4 ounces smoked salmon slices**

**6 free-range eggs**

**salt and freshly ground white pepper**

**2 tablespoons unsalted butter**

**2 tablespoons whipping cream**

**4 thick slices large baguette, cut on the angle, toasted and buttered while hot**

**1 1/2 teaspoons snipped fresh chives (optional)**

**1 1/2 teaspoons chopped fresh tarragon (optional)**

**1 1/2 teaspoons chopped fresh chervil (optional)**

Cut the smoked salmon slices into thin strips, removing any dark pieces as you go. Taste the smoked salmon at this stage. If it is very salted you will need to allow for this when you season your eggs.

Break the eggs into a bowl and whisk them with a little salt and pepper until they are well mixed. Make a bain-marie by placing a large frying pan over medium heat and pouring in about 1 1/2 inches of boiling water. Tip the eggs into a clean pan and place the pan in the bain-marie. Now this is where the patience is needed. Stir the eggs lazily with a wooden spoon (definitely not a whisk!), scraping the bottom of the pan as you go. The eggs will slowly form into soft, melting curds. Cook to the desired consistency, then remove the pan from the bain-marie and add the butter and cream. This addition of cold ingredients will stop the cooking and will keep the eggs at the desired consistency.

Serve the eggs spooned over the toasted baguette and sprinkled generously with the smoked salmon slices and herbs. Serve at once.

# Braised Lamb Shanks
## with Pearl Barley and Root Vegetables

THIS RECIPE IS FROM OUR FRIEND EUGENE CALLAGHAN IN GOREY, COUNTY WEXFORD. IT IS TYPICAL OF THE TASTY, HEARTY FARE THAT HE SERVES IN HIS PUB TO LOCALS AND VISITORS ALIKE. SHANKS ARE MEATY LEG JOINTS THAT ARE PERFECT FOR BRAISING. **Serves 4**

**4 lamb shanks**

**1 tablespoon vegetable oil**

**2 tablespoons pearl barley**

**1 1/4 cups lamb stock or water**

**1 fresh thyme sprig or 1/2 teaspoon dried thyme**

**1 fresh parsley sprig**

**1 teaspoon salt**

**5 ounces carrots, roughly chopped**

**1 large leek, cut into 8 pieces**

**4 small potatoes, quartered**

**2 small onions, quartered**

**salt and freshly ground black pepper**

**4 heaped tablespoons fresh parsley leaves, blanched and refreshed, to garnish**

Preheat the oven to 325°F.

Ask your butcher to trim off any excess fat and saw the knuckles from the shanks. Heat the oil in a large frying pan over high heat. Fry the lamb shanks until nicely colored on all sides. Transfer them to a large flameproof baking dish and add the barley, stock or water, herbs and salt. Cover tightly with foil and a lid and cook in the preheated oven for 1 1/2 hours.

Remove the casserole from the oven, add the vegetables and a little more water if necessary. Season the vegetables lightly with salt and pepper, then cover the dish and return it to the oven for a further hour.

Remove from the oven and check that the lamb is very tender and almost falling off the bone. If you think that it's not quite ready, return it to the oven for another 15 minutes.

Transfer the lamb to a warmed serving platter and cover while you finish the braised vegetables. Bring the dish back to a simmer on top of the stove, adding more water to give you a nice consistency if necessary. Add the blanched parsley leaves and check and adjust the seasoning to taste.

To serve, ladle the braised vegetables onto large warmed plates and place the shanks on top.

# Christmas Pudding Parfait

Have you ever wondered what to do with leftover Christmas pudding, especially when there's only a few portions remaining? This parfait is the perfect answer, and you'll be creating a simple and elegant dessert for New Year's Day or any special Yuletide gathering. We serve this with Brandied Apricot Sauce (see page 182), but it could be served with Vanilla Custard Sauce (see page 181) or brandy butter. **Serves 4** (V)

**2 1/2 ounces white chocolate, chopped**

**3/4 cup whipping cream**

**2 tablespoons milk**

**1/4 vanilla bean, split lengthwise**

**3 egg yolks**

**1 tablespoon superfine sugar**

**1 1/2 teaspoons brandy**

**6 ounces leftover Christmas pudding**

Place the white chocolate in a heatproof bowl over a pan of hot but not boiling water and leave to melt.

Place about half the cream, the milk and the vanilla bean in another pan and bring to a boil.

Whisk the egg yolks and the sugar together in a bowl until the sugar has dissolved. When the cream mixture has come to a boil, slowly pour it on to the yolk-sugar mixture, whisking continuously. Return to medium heat, heat to a gentle simmer, reduce the heat to low and cook, stirring continuously, until the custard is thick enough to coat the back of a spoon. When it is ready, strain into a mixing bowl and allow to cool slightly. Add the custard to the melted chocolate, not vice versa or the resulting mixture may not be as smooth. Beat together gently for about 10 minutes. Chill for 30 minutes.

Whip the remaining cream until it forms soft peaks, then fold it into the custard mixture along with the brandy.

Chop the Christmas pudding into rough crumb size, by hand or using the pulse on a food processor, and fold into the parfait mixture. It's important to have chopped it into as close to crumb consistency as possible; bigger chunks aren't as nice in the finished parfait.

Line a terrine or loaf pan with plastic wrap. Pour in the parfait, level the top and cover with plastic wrap. Leave to set in the refrigerator for at least 3 hours, or overnight if possible.

To serve, gently pull at the plastic wrap surround and the parfait should release from the mold with ease. Turn out onto a flat serving plate. Use a hot knife to cut a slice or two per portion. Arrange on individual plates.

CHAPTER FIVE

# Pub Grub

Pubs have always been a fundamental part of the social scene in Ireland: a place to gather, to share a drink, exchange a tale and refresh the spirit. When it comes to food, however, the unidentifiable lump of defrosted matter is no longer good enough. People are now looking for local specialities, food that is fresh and tasty and, of course, value for money. And why not? The possibilities are inexhaustible.

## Menu 1

Vegetable Chowder

Spicy Basil Mayonnaise

Ham Shanks with Horseradish Cream, Mushrooms and Peas

Derby Pie with Whipped Cream

## Menu 2

Shrimp, Avocado and Tomato Cocktail

Roast Chicken Drumsticks with Parsley and Garlic

Crusty Sautéed Potatoes

Lime Mousse with Marinated Kiwifruit

# Vegetable Chowder

WITH A PIECE OF CRUSTY BREAD AS AN ACCOMPANIMENT, A SOUP LIKE THIS IS A MEAL IN ITSELF. DON'T BE AFRAID TO LEAVE OUT A VEGETABLE IF YOU DON'T HAVE IT ON HAND, OR TO SUBSTITUTE ONE FOR ANOTHER. THIS SHOULD JUST BE A GUIDELINE TO START FROM. ZUCCHINI, PEAS, PUMPKIN AND FAVA BEANS ARE ALL POSSIBLE OPTIONS. **Serves 6** (V)

**1 1/3 cups finely chopped onion**

**1 1/3 cups finely chopped leeks**

**2 tablespoons oil or unsalted butter**

**3/4 cup finely chopped carrots**

**3/4 cup thinly sliced celery**

**2 garlic cloves, finely chopped**

**3 quarts vegetable stock**

**1 bouquet garni (leek, bay leaf, parsley, thyme, black peppercorns)**

**2 teaspoons salt**

**10 to 12 potatoes, peeled and cut into 1/2-inch dice**

**4 ounces green beans, blanched**

**1 1/4 cups sliced cabbage, blanched**

**1 can (14 ounces) diced tomatoes, undrained**

**1 cup macaroni**

**2/3 cup dried haricot beans, soaked overnight and cooked until soft**

**Spicy Basil Mayonnaise (see page 55) to serve**

In a large heavy-based pan, cook the onion and leeks in the oil or butter over medium heat for about 2 minutes. Add the carrots, celery and garlic and continue to cook for another 4 minutes, stirring occasionally, without allowing the vegetables to color.

Add the stock, bouquet garni and salt and bring to a boil. Add the potatoes, green beans, cabbage and tomatoes. Return to a boil and simmer gently for about 15 minutes. Add the pasta and continue to simmer for about 10 to 15 minutes, or until the pasta is cooked. At the last minute, gently stir in the cooked haricot beans.

To serve, ladle into warmed soup bowls. To finish the soup, scoop in a spoonful of Spicy Basil Mayonnaise. This soup keeps well for a couple of days in the refrigerator.

# Spicy Basil Mayonnaise

BY ADDING FLAVORS AND AROMAS SUCH AS THESE, MAYONNAISE IS GIVEN A NEW LEASE ON LIFE. JUST IMAGINE THE NEW DIMENSION THIS SPICY MAYONNAISE WILL ADD TO SOUPS, SALADS OR SANDWICHES.

**Makes about 1 3/4 cups** 

**2 egg yolks**

**pinch of ground red chili**

**4 garlic cloves, finely chopped**

**4 tablespoons light cream**

**1 1/3 cups chopped fresh basil leaves**

**1 1/8 cups light olive or vegetable oil**

**salt**

Place the egg yolks, chili, garlic, cream and basil in a blender or food processor. Blend or pulse for 20 seconds. Stop and scrap down the sides with a spatula. Blend or process again, and with the machine running, slowly and steadily pour in the oil. Check and adjust the seasoning to taste, adding salt as necessary. This mayonnaise will keep in the refrigerator for about 3 days.

# Ham Shanks
## with Horseradish Cream, Mushrooms and Peas

THIS IS THE TYPE OF DISH THAT WILL MAKE YOU LOOK LIKE A PROFESSIONAL IN THE KITCHEN. THE HAM SHANKS CAN BE PREPARED UP TO 2 DAYS IN ADVANCE AND THE SAUCE IS A GREAT, NO-FUSS WINNER. GET READY TO IMPRESS! YOU CAN FINISH THE DISH UNDER THE BROILER IF YOU WISH. GENTLY STIR A FURTHER 1/2 CUP OF WHIPPED CREAM INTO THE FINISHED SAUCE, LEAVING IT IN LARGE CURDS. SERVE THE HAM ON FLAMEPROOF PLATES, SPOON THE SAUCE OVER THE HAM AND GLAZE EACH PLATE UNDER A PREHEATED MEDIUM BROILER FOR ABOUT 1 MINUTE. THE CURDS OF WHIPPED CREAM WILL BROWN TO GIVE A WONDERFUL GOLDEN FINISH. **Serves 6**

**3 ham shanks, about 2 pounds each**

For the sauce:

**3 tablespoons unsalted butter**

**3 shallots or green onions, finely chopped**

**6 ounces mushrooms, thinly sliced**

**salt**

**2 tablespoons dry sherry**

**1 1/2 cups whipping cream**

**1 cup shelled peas**

**2 to 3 tablespoons bottled horseradish**

**freshly ground black pepper**

**chopped fresh parsley to garnish**

Put the shanks in a large pan of cold water. Bring to a boil, simmer for 2 minutes, then refresh under cold water. Cover again with cold water and bring to the boil. Skim off any scum that rises to the surface, cover with a lid and simmer for 2 1/2 to 3 hours, or until the meat is very tender. Transfer the shanks to a clean bowl and allow to cool. When they are cool enough to handle, remove and discard the skin. Flake the meat off the bone and cut into 3/4- to 1 1/4-inch chunks.

To make the sauce, heat a large pan over medium heat. Melt the butter and cook the shallots or green onions and mushrooms for 3 minutes with a little salt. Add the sherry and bring to a boil. Add the cream and peas and boil vigorously until the cream thickens.

To serve, warm the pieces of ham in a covered pan with a little of the cooking liquid or in your microwave on full power for 3 minutes. Bring the sauce to a boil and add the horseradish. Do not boil again or you will spoil the flavor of the horseradish. Season to taste with salt and pepper. Spoon the ham shanks into warmed bowls, cover generously with sauce and sprinkle with parsley.

# Derby Pie
## with Whipped Cream

THIS TASTY YET EASY-TO-MAKE PIE ORIGINATES IN THE DEEP SOUTHERN STATES OF AMERICA. TO US, PECANS, CHOCOLATE AND BOURBON GO TOGETHER LIKE PEAS IN A POD. IT IS BEST MADE IN A 9-INCH PAN.

**Serves 8 to 10** 

- **9 ounces Shortcrust Pastry (see page 177)**
- **1 cup pecans, chopped**
- **4 eggs**
- **2/3 cup superfine sugar**
- **2/3 cup all-purpose flour**
- **1/2 cup unsalted butter, melted**
- **2 tablespoons bourbon**
- **1 teaspoon vanilla extract**
- **3/4 cup chocolate chips**
- **whipped cream to serve**

Preheat the oven to 350°F.

Roll out the pastry to a thickness of about 1/4 inch and use to line an ovenproof 9-inch cast-iron frying pan. Chill in the refrigerator for at least 30 minutes.

Lightly toast the pecans by placing them on a baking sheet and putting in the preheated oven for about 5 to 10 minutes. Leave to cool.

In a large bowl, whisk together the eggs and sugar until the sugar has dissolved. Stir in the flour, butter, bourbon and vanilla extract. Fold in the chocolate chips and pecan pieces. Pour the filling into the unbaked pie shell and place in the preheated oven for about 40 minutes, or until golden.

Serve warm, with a generous dollop of whipped cream.

# Shrimp, Avocado and Tomato Cocktail

HERE WE HAVE A VERY SIMPLE BUT PERFECT LITTLE SHRIMP OR PRAWN COCKTAIL—YOU CAN MAKE IT WITH EITHER—THAT WE LIKE TO PRESENT IN THE SAME FASHION AS THE ROMAINE SALAD BOATS (SEE PAGE 34).

**Serves 4**

**12 ounces cooked and peeled shrimp or prawns**

**1 avocado, peeled and diced**

**8 red cherry tomatoes, quartered**

**8 yellow cherry tomatoes, quartered**

**salt and freshly ground black pepper**

**12 little green lettuce leaves**

**fresh cilantro sprigs to garnish**

For the sauce:

**6 tablespoons plain yogurt**

**6 tablespoons mayonnaise**

**2 tablespoons tomato ketchup**

**1/2 teaspoon chili powder**

**2 tablespoons chopped fresh cilantro**

Make the sauce by whisking together all the ingredients in a small bowl. If you're making the sauce in advance don't add the cilantro until the last moment. Without the herb, the sauce will keep for 4 to 5 days in the refrigerator.

To assemble, gently toss together the shrimp or prawns, avocado and tomatoes with half the sauce. Add a little salt and some freshly ground pepper. Now trim flat the main rib on the back of each salad leaf so that the leaves will sit on the plate without rolling over. Put a spoonful of sauce on the middle of each plate. (This will stop the leaves from sliding around.) Fill each salad leaf with the shrimp or prawn mixture and arrange 3 leaves on each plate. Garnish with a sprig of cilantro and serve.

# Roast Chicken Drumsticks
## with Parsley and Garlic

DRUMSTICKS ARE A GREAT SNACK FOOD. THEY HAVE A DELICIOUS RICH TEXTURE THAT DOESN'T DRY OUT ON REHEATING. THEY'RE CHEAP AND EASY TO BUY, AND KIDS LIKE THEM, TOO. PAUL'S A BIG FAN, ESPECIALLY OF THIS RECIPE, WHICH REMINDS HIM OF HIS FIRST TRIP TO FRANCE. THAT'S BECAUSE OF THE PARSLEY AND GARLIC, OR *PERSILLADE* AS THE FRENCH CALL IT. **Serves 4**

**12 to 16 chicken drumsticks**

**salt and freshly ground black pepper**

**1 tablespoon olive oil**

**4 tablespoons butter**

**3 garlic cloves, finely chopped**

**2 tablespoons chopped fresh parsley**

**1 tablespoon lemon juice**

Season the chicken generously with salt and pepper. Heat a large, heavy pan over medium heat with the oil and half the butter. When the butter is foaming, add the chicken and cook until lightly browned.

Cover with a lid and cook over gentle heat for a further 25 minutes, turning the drumsticks frequently during this period and monitoring the heat so that they fry gently. Add the remaining butter with the garlic, parsley and lemon juice and allow to infuse off the heat for a few minutes before serving.

# Crusty Sautéed Potatoes

EVERYONE SEEMS TO LOVE THESE SAUTÉED POTATOES. THE SECRET IS IN THE POTATO, WHICH MUST BE FLOURY TO GIVE THE RIGHT CRUSTY TEXTURE. FOR THE RESTAURANT, WE COOK UP A LARGE BATCH OF SPUDS, THEN PEEL AND FRY THEM AS NEEDED. **Serves 4** (V)

**2 pounds floury potatoes**

**1 tablespoon salt**

**6 tablespoons vegetable oil**

**3 tablespoons butter**

For the spiced salt:

**1/2 teaspoon salt**

**1 teaspoon garlic salt**

**1 teaspoon dried thyme**

**1 teaspoon paprika**

Put the potatoes in a large pan with the salt and cover with cold water. Bring to a boil, then simmer gently for about 15 to 20 minutes, or until cooked. Drain and allow to cool. Peel off the skins with a knife and slice about 1/2 inch thick.

Unless you have a huge frying pan or 2 pans to work with, it's much better to fry these in two batches. Heat your frying pan over high heat. Add half the oil and butter and allow the butter to foam. Add half the potatoes and fry on each side until golden and well crusted. Mix together the spiced salt ingredients and season the potatoes with a little of the mixture. Cook for a further 1 minute, then drain on paper towels. If you are cooking in batches, keep the first batch warm in the oven while you prepare the second batch, using the remaining oil and butter.

# Lime Mousse
## with Marinated Kiwifruit

THIS LIME MOUSSE IS SUBLIME—FEATHERLIGHT AND TASTE-BUD TANTALIZING! IT COULD EASILY BE PAIRED WITH MANGO OR PAPAYA IF PREFERRED, OR EVEN THE EXOTIC FRUIT SALAD (SEE PAGE 112).

**Serves 4 to 6** 

**1 1/2 teaspoons powdered gelatin**

**juice of 4 limes**

**4 eggs, separated**

**2/3 cup superfine sugar**

**finely grated zest of 2 limes**

**3/4 cup whipping cream**

**4 to 6 kiwifruits**

**1/2 quantity Lime-Ginger Syrup (see page 112)**

**candied lime, cut into julienne strips**

**fresh mint sprigs**

In a small pan, soften the gelatin in the lime juice for 5 minutes, then place over low heat until the gelatin dissolves. Set aside.

In a bowl over a pan of simmering water, whisk together the egg yolks with a scant 1/2 cup of the sugar for about 5 minutes until the mixture is thick and pale and trails off the whisk in ribbons. Remove from the heat and add the mixture, dissolved gelatin and lime zest. Set the bowl over a bowl of iced water and continue to whisk gently until cold and starting to set. Whip the cream until it forms soft peaks. Whisk 2 of the egg whites (save the other two for another recipe) until they form soft peaks. Add the remaining sugar and whisk until glossy and firm.

Fold the whipped cream into the lime mixture. Fold in the egg whites. Taste to check the tartness, and add a little more lime juice if necessary. Pour into a serving bowl and leave to set in the refrigerator for at least 4 hours.

Peel the kiwifruits and slice or cut into wedges. Ten minutes before serving, toss in the Lime-Ginger Syrup.

To serve, use an ice cream scoop or large spoon to place 2 scoops of the lime mousse on individual plates. Using a slotted spoon, arrange some kiwifruit pieces around the mousse. Decorate with candied lime julienne and mint if desired.

OVERLEAF:

Pub Grub, Menu 2

SOLINGEN

CHAPTER SIX

# Country Fare

To many people, country fare may suggest simple one-pot dishes, but to us it implies much more: regional specialties, family secrets passed down through the generations, and a delight in using locally available fresh produce. It takes us back to the days of self-sufficiency and living off the land.

### Menu 1

Fried Pollen or Trout in Oatmeal with Tomato and Sorrel Cream

Grilled Whole Pollen or Trout with Sorrel Purée

Marinated Loin of Pork with Thyme

Candied Shallots

Pear and Walnut Upside-Down Cake

### Menu 2

Old-Fashioned Salmon Mayonnaise

Melba Toast

Haunch of Venison with Red Wine, Black Pepper and Thyme

Celeriac Purée

Spiced Banana Cake with Bourbon Cream

# Fried Pollen or Trout in Oatmeal
## with Tomato and Sorrel Cream

POLLEN IS A FRESHWATER FISH THAT SEEMS TO BE PECULIAR TO ONLY A FEW LAKES IN IRELAND. IT'S SOMETIMES CALLED THE FRESHWATER HERRING, BUT WE FEEL THAT IT'S CLOSER TO TROUT IN TEXTURE AND FLAVOR. FEEL FREE TO SUBSTITUTE TROUT IN THESE RECIPES. IF YOU PREFER A HEAVIER COATING ON THE FISH, DIP THE FILLETS IN A MIXTURE OF 1 EGG BEATEN WITH 6 TABLESPOONS OF MILK BEFORE YOU ROLL THEM IN THE OATS. **Serves 4**

**3 cups rolled oats**

**8 to 12 pollen or trout fillets, scaled but skin on**

**salt and freshly ground white pepper**

**3 tablespoons vegetable oil**

**2 tablespoons unsalted butter**

For the sauce:

**1 tablespoon butter**

**1 cup finely shredded sorrel leaves**

**1 large plum tomato, peeled, seeded and diced**

**3/4 cup plus 2 tablespoons whipping cream**

To cook the fish, first spread the oats on a large plate. Season the fish fillets lightly with salt and pepper, then roll them in the oats. Press the oats on to each fillet with your hands. Heat a large frying pan over medium heat and add half of the oil and butter. Wait until the butter is foaming, then add 4 to 6 fish fillets and fry for 2 minutes on each side. If you are cooking in batches, transfer the fish to a baking sheet lined with paper towels and keep them warm in a low oven while you cook the rest.

To make the sauce, melt the butter in a small pan over gentle heat. As the butter is melting, add the sorrel, tomato and a little salt and white pepper. Cook gently for about 2 minutes, then add the cream. Turn up the heat a little and bring the cream to a boil. Boil gently until the cream thickens to sauce consistency, stirring occasionally. Remove from the heat, check and adjust the seasoning to taste.

To serve, lay the fillets on warmed plates and surround with a few spoonfuls of sauce.

OVERLEAF:

Country Fare, Menu 1

Fried Pollen or Trout in Oatmeal with Tomato and Sorrel Cream (page 65)

Marinated Loin of Pork with Thyme (page 69)

Candied Shallots (page 70)

Pear and Walnut Upside-Down Cake (page 71)

# Grilled Whole Pollen or Trout
## with Sorrel Purée

PAUL HAS OFTEN LAMENTED THAT WE DON'T GET CERTAIN FISH IN OUR LOCAL WATERS, SUCH AS SARDINES. BUT WHEN HE TRIED CHARCOAL-GRILLED POLLEN, HE REALIZED THAT WE DIDN'T NEED THEM ANYWAY. THE GRILLING CRISPS THE SKIN AND HEIGHTENS THE FLAVORS SO THAT THE FISH STANDS UP BEAUTIFULLY TO THE TANGY SORREL PURÉE. BY THE WAY, FEEL FREE TO SUBSTITUTE SARDINES OR TROUT! IT IS A SHAME THAT SORREL TURNS A GREEN-GRAY WHEN COOKED. COOKS OFTEN TRY TO KEEP THE COLOR BY COOKING IT LESS. THIS WORKS TO A CERTAIN EXTENT, BUT WE'VE ALWAYS FOUND THAT THE FLAVORS ARE CLEARER AND LESS ACIDIC WHEN THE SORREL LEAVES ARE PROPERLY COOKED. THIS IS AN EXCELLENT ALTERNATIVE TO THE FRIED POLLEN OR TROUT IN OATMEAL (SEE PAGE 65). **Serves 4**

**8 whole pollen or trout, scaled and gutted**

**1 tablespoon vegetable oil**

**salt and freshly ground black pepper**

For the sorrel purée:

**2 tablespoons unsalted butter**

**12 ounces sorrel leaves, stemmed and roughly chopped**

**2/3 cup whipping cream**

Preheat the barbecue or broiler.

Make sure that the fish are dry or they will stick to the grill. Drizzle the fish with the oil and rub it into the fish evenly. Season lightly with salt and pepper. Place on the barbecue and grill for 2 to 3 minutes on each side. If you're using a broiler, cover a baking sheet with lightly oiled foil and broil the fish for about 6 minutes, turning once during the cooking time.

To make the sorrel purée, warm a large pan over medium heat. Melt the butter in the pan, then add the sorrel. Cook the sorrel with a little salt for about 2 minutes. Add the cream and bring to a boil. Boil gently until the cream thickens slightly, then purée in a blender or food processor. Check and season to taste, then serve.

# Marinated Loin of Pork
## with Thyme

Here we give the pork roast a long marinade so that it takes on a taste similar to wild boar. This is one of the first recipes that Paul ever cooked (even before he turned professional), and it's still one that we come back to. **Serves 4**

**1 rack of pork, about 2 1/2 pounds**

**2 tablespoons vegetable oil**

**2 tablespoons unsalted butter, diced**

**salt and freshly ground black pepper**

For the marinade:

**2 garlic cloves, crushed**

**1 carrot, diced**

**1 onion, diced**

**7 tablespoons red wine vinegar**

**1 1/4 cups red wine**

**4 tablespoons olive oil**

**1 teaspoon black peppercorns**

**1 1/2 tablespoons salt**

**1 teaspoon sugar**

**2 bay leaves**

**4 fresh thyme sprigs**

**12 juniper berries**

Preheat the oven to 400°F.

Remove the skin of the pork if your butcher has not already done so. Place all the marinade ingredients in a large pan and bring to a boil. Simmer for 2 minutes, then allow to cool. Place the pork in a deep nonreactive (ceramic or stainless steel) container and pour the marinade over the pork. Cover with plastic wrap and chill for 48 hours, turning every 6 hours.

After 48 hours, remove the pork from the marinade and dry with a clean cloth. Reserve the marinade. Heat a large frying pan over high heat, add the oil and brown the pork on all sides. Transfer the pork to a roasting pan and place in the preheated oven for 40 minutes. Remove the roast from the oven and place the pork to rest on a large plate lightly covered with foil.

Drain any excess fat from the pan and deglaze it over high heat using 3/4 cup plus 2 tablespoons of the marinade liquid. Scrape the bottom of the pan with a wooden spoon to loosen all the delicious caramelized juices. Strain into a clean pan and boil until you have reduced the liquid by about half.

Now whisk in the diced butter and check and adjust the seasoning to taste.

Carve the pork into equal portions and serve with a little sauce.

# Candied Shallots

THESE SIMPLE LITTLE BEAUTIES SEEM TO LIFT ANY ROAST MEAT INTO A HIGHER REALM. **Serves 4** 

**24 shallots**

**3 tablespoons unsalted butter**

**1 tablespoon vegetable oil**

**2 tablespoons sugar**

**3/4 cup plus 2 tablespoons red wine or pork marinade (see page 69)**

Peel the shallots carefully, leaving the root intact to keep the shallots together. It's also nice to leave the wispy pointed ends on because they are so attractive.

Heat a large frying pan over medium heat. Add the butter and oil. When the butter is foaming, add the shallots and fry gently until they turn golden in color. Add the sugar and continue to cook for about 3 minutes, or until the sugar begins to caramelize. Add the red wine or marinade, cover with a lid and cook gently for 10 minutes. Remove the lid and boil off any excess liquid so that the shallots become beautifully candied.

# Pear and Walnut Upside-Down Cake

UPSIDE-DOWN CAKES LIKE THIS ARE A TRADITIONAL FAVORITE IN THE UNITED STATES. MANY PEOPLE USE CANNED PINEAPPLE RINGS, BUT WE PREFER A FRESH FRUIT SUCH AS PEAR OR APPLE. A CARAMEL OR TOFFEE SAUCE ENHANCES THIS DESSERT, BUT SIMPLE WHIPPED CREAM MAKES IT LOVELY, TOO. **Serves 6 to 8** (V)

**1/2 cup plus 3 tablespoons unsalted butter, melted**

**3/4 cup superfine sugar**

**3/4 cup firmly packed light brown sugar**

**4 to 6 ripe pears**

**1 cup walnut halves**

For the cake batter:

**3/4 cup unsalted butter, softened**

**1 2/3 cups superfine sugar**

**1 3/4 cups all-purpose flour**

**1 1/2 tablespoons baking powder**

**1/2 teaspoon baking soda**

**2 1/4 teaspoons salt**

**1 teaspoon ground cinnamon**

**1/2 teaspoon ground cloves**

**1/2 teaspoon freshly grated nutmeg**

**3 eggs**

**1 cup buttermilk**

**whipped cream to serve**

Preheat the oven to 350°F and grease a 10-inch round or square cake pan.

Pour the melted butter into the cake pan. Add the superfine and light brown sugar and stir together with a fork until all the sugar has mixed into the butter. Set aside.

Peel, halve and core the pears. Arrange attractively, curved side down, in the melted butter-sugar mixture in the cake pan. Place walnut halves among the pears, filling in any gaps.

To make the cake batter, cream together the butter and sugar until light and fluffy. Sift together all the dry ingredients. Break and lightly stir the eggs together. Add the eggs slowly to the butter-sugar mixture, making sure each addition is fully incorporated before adding more.

By hand, alternately fold in one-quarter of the dry ingredients followed by one-third of the buttermilk. Continue adding the rest until all is well mixed together. Pour this batter over the pears in the cake pan and bake in the preheated oven for about 40 minutes, or until the cake is coming away from the sides of the pan and a skewer inserted in the center comes out clean. Remove from the oven and leave to cool for at least 10 minutes. Loosen the cake from the sides with a sharp knife and invert the cake pan onto a rimmed plate. Most of the pan juices will have been absorbed by the pears, but if there are any left, spoon them over the cake.

Serve the cake warm, sliced into individual portions and arranged on warmed plates, with whipped cream on the side.

# Old-Fashioned Salmon Mayonnaise

SALMON MAYONNAISE HAS BEEN SERVED IN IRISH COUNTRY HOUSES AND RESTAURANTS FOR GENERATIONS. ALTHOUGH IT KEEPS WELL IN THE REFRIGERATOR, WE FEEL THAT IT IS AT ITS VERY BEST NEVER HAVING SEEN THE REFRIGERATOR, AND SERVED FRESHLY MADE AT ROOM TEMPERATURE WITH LOTS OF MELBA TOAST (SEE PAGE 73). **Serves 4**

For the poaching liquid:

**2/3 cup dry white wine**

**1 tablespoon vinegar**

**1 1/4 cups water**

**6 peppercorns**

**1 fresh parsley sprig**

**2 teaspoons salt**

**1 pound fresh salmon fillet, skinned**

**5 tablespoons mayonnaise**

**2 teaspoons Dijon mustard**

**1 1/2 teaspoons finely chopped gherkins**

**1 1/2 teaspoons chopped capers**

**1 1/2 teaspoons chopped fresh dill**

**1 1/2 teaspoons snipped fresh chives**

To garnish:

**a few salad leaves**

**a few fresh dill sprigs**

Combine the ingredients for the poaching liquid in a small pan and bring to a boil. Meanwhile, check the salmon for bones. Cut off any brown flesh and cut into 6 to 8 cubes. Add the salmon to the poaching liquid and simmer for 3 minutes. Remove the pan from the heat and allow to cool.

Using a slotted spoon, remove the salmon from the pan and place in a medium-sized bowl, keeping the flakes large and generously sized. Fold in the remaining ingredients, garnish with salad leaves and dill, and serve at room temperature.

# Melba Toast

MELBA TOAST IS A GREAT ACCOMPANIMENT TO ALMOST ANY FIRST COURSE. IT'S ALSO GOOD FUN TO MAKE, ESPECIALLY FOR KIDS. IN OUR EXPERIENCE MOST PEOPLE LOVE MELBA TOAST, SO MAKE LOTS!

**Serves 4** 

**4 to 6 slices of bread, each about 1/2 inch thick**

Trim the crusts off the bread slices and toast on both sides. Cut each slice in half on the diagonal. Set flat on a board and carefully cut between the two toasted sides of each slice. Set on a baking sheet cut side up until required.

Preheat the broiler.

Finish the toast under the broiler on a low shelf until crisp and warm.

# Haunch of Venison
## with Red Wine, Black Pepper and Thyme

THE HAUNCH IS SIMPLY THE LEG OF AN ANIMAL, AND WITH THE LOIN OF VENISON BEING SO EXPENSIVE, THE HAUNCH IS A SUPER ALTERNATIVE. ASK YOUR BUTCHER FOR A PIECE FROM THE TOP OF THE LEG, WHICH WILL BE A LITTLE MORE TENDER. **Serves 4**

**1 3/4 pounds boneless venison leg meat**

**salt**

**2 tablespoons black peppercorns, cracked**

**1 tablespoon vegetable oil**

**5 tablespoons butter, chilled and diced**

**1 1/2 teaspoons fresh thyme leaves or 1/2 teaspoon dried thyme**

**1 1/4 cups red wine**

**sugar**

**fresh thyme sprigs to garnish**

Preheat the oven to 350°F.

Have your butcher trim the venison of as much sinew as possible. It would be ideal if he could "seam out" an entire muscle, which would give you a piece of meat that would be entirely sinew-free. Season the venison generously with salt. Press all but 1 teaspoon of the black pepper into the meat.

Heat a heavy ovenproof frying pan over medium heat. Add the oil and 2 tablespoons of butter. Allow the butter to foam, then add the venison. Brown the meat on all sides, then place in the oven. It is difficult to predict exactly how long it will take to cook because the leg meat can be many different shapes, so use these cooking times as a guideline. If you have a long, thin piece, it should take about 10 minutes for rare and 16 for medium to well done. A short, stubby piece should take about 15 minutes for rare and 25 minutes for medium to well done. We don't recommend venison cooked more than medium well as it will tend to be very dry. When cooked, transfer the meat to a warmed plate, cover it with foil and allow it to rest while you make the sauce.

Pour any fat out of the pan and add the thyme, the remaining pepper and the red wine. Boil until only 6 tablespoons of liquid remain, then remove the pan from the heat and whisk in the remaining cold diced butter. This will mellow and thicken the sauce. Taste the sauce for seasoning and add a little sugar and salt if necessary.

Carve the venison into 1/2-inch slices, adding any juices to the sauce. Arrange on warmed plates, garnish each with a sprig of thyme and pour over a little sauce.

# Celeriac Purée

THIS PURÉE IS A GREAT ALTERNATIVE TO MASHED POTATOES. IT GOES WONDERFULLY WELL WITH ALL GAME, BEEF AND PORK. **Serves 4 to 6** (V)

Place the celeriac, potatoes, salt and water in a medium pan. Cover tightly and bring to a boil. Reduce the heat and simmer very gently for about 15 to 20 minutes, or until the potatoes and celeriac are cooked. Drain into a colander, then return them to the pan with the butter and cream. Bring to a boil, and boil until the cream thickens slightly, stirring frequently because it has a tendency to catch on the bottom. Purée in a blender or food processor until smooth. Season to taste with salt and pepper.

**1 celeriac, about 2 pounds, peeled and roughly chopped**

**9 ounces potatoes, peeled and roughly chopped**

**1 1/2 teaspoons salt**

**2 1/4 cups water**

**2 tablespoons butter**

**1 1/4 cups whipping cream**

**salt and freshly ground white pepper**

# Spiced Banana Cake
## with Bourbon Cream

THERE'S SOMETHING EXTREMELY COMFORTING ABOUT MOIST CAKES LIKE THIS. IT TASTES DELICIOUS AS A DESSERT AND YOU CAN SAVE THE REST FOR AFTERNOON TEA. **Serves 8 to 10** (V)

**1 1/4 cups all-purpose flour**

**1 cup golden raisins**

**1 cup pecans, toasted and chopped**

**3/4 teaspoon ground cinnamon**

**1/2 teaspoon freshly grated nutmeg**

**1/4 to 1/2 teaspoon salt**

**2 teaspoons baking powder**

**3 ripe bananas**

**1/2 cup bourbon**

**3 eggs**

**1/2 cup plus 1 tablespoon unsalted butter**

**1 1/4 cups superfine sugar**

**1 3/4 cups whipping cream, softly whipped**

**1 cup Toffee Sauce (see page 184) to serve**

Preheat the oven to 375°F. Grease a 9-inch springform pan and line the bottom with parchment paper.

Take 2 tablespoons flour and toss the raisins and pecans in it. This helps keep the fruit from sinking to the bottom of the batter.

In a bowl, sift together the remaining flour, spices, salt and baking powder. Mash the bananas to a rough pulp with half the bourbon. Break the eggs and stir together gently. Whisk together the butter and 1 cup of the sugar until light and fluffy. Gradually mix in the mashed banana. Slowly, mayonnaise-style, add the eggs, making sure they are fully incorporated. Fold in the dry ingredients, and finally the flour-coated fruit and nuts. Pour into the prepared cake pan and cook in the preheated oven for about 1 hour, or until a skewer inserted in the center comes out clean. Remove from the oven and leave to cool. Remove from the pan.

Fold the remaining sugar and bourbon into the softly whipped cream.

To serve, place a slice of cake on each plate. Place a spoonful of bourbon cream alongside and drizzle both with Toffee Sauce.

CHAPTER SEVEN

# Meals from the Market

Market shopping is really about finding out what is available on the day. It's a fun way to shop because the marketplace pervades all the senses, with its smells, colors and sounds, while the vendors try to lure you into buying their wares.

## Menu 1

Crubeens Sausage with a Mustard Crust and Sweet Peppers

Glazed Monkfish with Black Pepper and Ginger

Poached White Peaches with Raspberry Sauce

## Menu 2

Seviche with Tomato, Lime and Cilantro

Stir-Fried Vegetable Frittata

Strawberry and Mascarpone Torte

# Crubeens Sausage
## with a Mustard Crust and Sweet Peppers

CRUBEENS IS THE NAME USED IN IRELAND FOR PIGS' TROTTERS, AND TO MOST PEOPLE IT SOUNDS A LOT MORE APPETIZING. THIS IS A DISH THAT WE DEVELOPED TO ENCOURAGE CUSTOMERS TO TRY TROTTERS IN THE RESTAURANT, AND IT WORKS VERY WELL. **Serves 4**

**1 pig's trotter**

**4 cups beef or chicken stock or water, or as needed to cover**

**1 leek, roughly chopped**

**1 onion, roughly chopped**

**1 carrot, roughly chopped**

**1 bouquet garni (leek, bay leaf, parsley, thyme, black peppercorns)**

**2 red bell peppers**

**2 yellow bell peppers**

**2 tablespoons vegetable oil**

**7 ounces coarse bulk sausage meat**

**2 1/2 tablespoons whole-grain mustard**

**2 cups coarse fresh bread crumbs**

**2 teaspoons butter, melted**

**1 tablespoon chopped fresh parsley**

**salt and freshly ground black pepper**

Put the pig's trotter in a large pot and add stock or water to cover. Bring to a boil over medium heat and skim off any scum that rises to the surface. Add the vegetables and the bouquet garni, cover and simmer slowly for about 4 hours. Remove the trotter from the liquid and allow to cool. Reserve the liquid. When cool enough to handle, flake all the meat from the bones and chop it into 1/2-inch dice. Reserve.

Preheat the oven to 400°F.

While the trotter is cooling, rub the peppers with a tablespoon of oil and roast in the hot oven or under the broiler until well blistered. Allow the peppers to cool, then peel, seed and cut into thin strips.

To make the sausage patties, simply combine the sausage meat with the chopped crubeens. With your hands, firm it into patties about 2 1/2 inches in diameter. Heat a heavy ovenproof frying pan over medium heat, add the remaining oil and fry the sausage patties for 2 minutes on one side. Turn them over and brush each one generously with the mustard. Sprinkle with bread crumbs and top with a little melted butter. If your frying pan fits into the oven, put it in. If not, transfer the patties to a roasting pan and pop them in the preheated oven for 10 minutes, or until they are firm to the touch and have a golden brown crust. Carefully transfer each one to a warmed serving plate. Add the sliced peppers to the frying pan to deglaze all those tasty caramelized juices. Add about 6 tablespoons of the poaching stock and the parsley and bring to a boil. Season with salt and pepper and serve at once with the sausage patties.

# Glazed Monkfish
## with Black Pepper and Ginger

THE FIRM TEXTURE AND GOOD FLAVOR OF MONKFISH MAKE IT AN IDEAL CANDIDATE FOR THIS RECIPE. OTHER OPTIONS MIGHT BE SHARK, TURBOT OR LING, BUT WE FIND MOST PEOPLE ADORE MONKFISH. IT'S AN EXCITING ONE-PAN DISH WHERE THE FLAVORS FROM THE EAST MEET SOME FINE FRESH PRODUCE FROM THE WEST. AN EXCELLENT ACCOMPANIMENT FOR THIS IS SOME CRISP SHREDDED CABBAGE STIR-FRIED WITH SHIITAKE MUSHROOMS. **Serves 4**

**4 monkfish fillets, 7 ounces each**

**salt**

**1/4 cup black peppercorns, cracked**

**2 tablespoons vegetable oil**

**1 tablespoon butter**

**2 teaspoons peeled and grated fresh ginger**

**2 teaspoons soft brown sugar**

**1 teaspoon black peppercorns, cracked**

**1/4 cup Japanese soy sauce**

**3 tablespoons rice wine vinegar**

**7 tablespoons whipping cream**

**2 tablespoons chopped fresh cilantro**

Ask your fishmonger to trim the monkfish fillets properly so that they are ready to cook.

Season each fillet lightly with salt and roll each one in the 1/4 cup peppercorns, pushing the pepper into the flesh. Heat a frying pan over medium heat. Add the oil and butter and heat until the butter is foaming. Add the monkfish fillets and fry for 4 to 5 minutes on each side. Add the ginger and fry for 30 seconds. Next add the sugar, 1 teaspoon pepper, soy sauce and rice wine vinegar and boil rapidly to reduce the liquids to a nice glaze. Roll the monkfish in the glaze and transfer to a warmed serving plate.

Add the cream and the cilantro to the sauce and boil until the cream thickens to sauce consistency. Serve with the monkfish.

# Poached White Peaches
## with Raspberry Sauce

WHITE PEACHES EPITOMIZE SUMMER FRUIT. SEDUCTIVELY SCENTED, WITH SWEET JUICY FLESH, SOMETHING THIS PERFECT NEEDS LITTLE MEDDLING WITH. THE RASPBERRY SAUCE COULD EASILY BE SUBSTITUTED BY STRAWBERRY OR BLACKBERRY IF PREFERRED. TO REALLY DRESS UP THE PRESENTATION, USE TWO OR THREE FRUIT SAUCES AS WE DID ON THE TELEVISION SHOW. THE POACHING LIQUID STORES INDEFINITELY IN THE REFRIGERATOR. **Serves 4** (V)

**2 cups water**

**2 1/2 cups superfine sugar**

**1 1/2 cups good quality sparkling wine**

**1/2 lemon**

**1 vanilla bean, split lengthwise**

**4 ripe, unblemished white peaches**

For the raspberry sauce:

**1 pint (2 cups) fresh or frozen raspberries**

**7 tablespoons water**

**1/2 to 2/3 cup superfine sugar**

**1 tablespoon lemon juice**

**fresh mint sprigs to decorate**

Place the water, sugar, sparkling wine, lemon and vanilla bean in a pan and bring to a boil, stirring to dissolve the sugar.

With a very sharp knife, make a little cross-cut incision at the top of each peach. Gently place the peaches in the poaching liquid, cover with parchment paper and simmer gently for 5 to 10 minutes, depending upon the ripeness of the peaches. A knife will go through the flesh with no resistance when they are cooked. Remove from the heat and leave the peaches to cool in the syrup.

To make the sauce, place the raspberries, water, sugar and lemon juice in a blender or food processor, and purée. Pass through a fine sieve and taste. Adjust if necessary with more lemon or sugar, depending on the sweetness of the berries.

With a sharp knife, delicately peel the skins off the peaches. They are now ready to use or can be stored in the syrup in the refrigerator for up to 10 days.

To serve, ladle a generous spoonful of the raspberry sauce onto the center of each plate. Place a drained peach in the center, and decorate with fresh mint.

# Seviche

## with Tomato, Lime and Cilantro

SEVICHE IS THE TYPE OF DISH THAT YOU SHOULD MAKE ON MARKET DAY BECAUSE IT REQUIRES REALLY FRESH FISH. ASK YOUR FISHMONGER FOR WHATEVER IS FRESHEST. ANY FISH CAN BE USED, BUT SALMON, HAKE, TURBOT, SCALLOPS, MACKEREL AND HALIBUT ARE SOME OF OUR FAVORITES. **Serves 4**

**5 ounces very fresh hake fillet, skinned**

**5 ounces very fresh salmon fillet, skinned**

**2/3 cup fresh lime juice**

**1 teaspoon salt**

**freshly ground black pepper**

**2 ripe tomatoes, peeled, seeded and diced**

**2 tablespoons thinly sliced red onion**

**2 to 4 fresh chilies, seeded and thinly sliced**

**1 small avocado, peeled and diced**

**3 tablespoons chopped fresh cilantro**

**2 tablespoons olive oil**

To garnish:

**finely sliced salad leaves**

**fresh cilantro sprigs**

Check the fish for any bones and cut into fine slices or 1/2-inch dice. In a ceramic or stainless steel bowl, combine the fish with the lime juice, salt and pepper. Cover and chill for 2 hours, stirring occasionally.

Remove from the refrigerator, add the remaining ingredients and allow to marinate for 30 minutes. Taste for seasoning, adding more salt and chili if preferred. Serve on a "nest" of sliced lettuce and top with a sprig of fresh cilantro.

OVERLEAF:

# Stir-Fried Vegetable Frittata

THE WONDERFUL THING ABOUT FRITTATAS IS THEIR VERSATILITY. THEY ARE BASICALLY JUST THE ITALIAN VERSION OF A ONE-PAN OMELET, RATHER LIKE A SPANISH OMELET, AND ARE NORMALLY MADE WITH WHATEVER IS ON HAND, IN SEASON OR AT THE MARKET. YOU CAN ALSO SERVE THIS RECIPE WITH CRUSTY SAUTÉED POTATOES (SEE PAGE 60) AND SALAD OF HERBS (SEE PAGE 169). **Serves 4** (V)

**1 tablespoon olive oil**

**2 tablespoons unsalted butter**

**1 red bell pepper, seeded and thinly sliced**

**5 ounces mushrooms, sliced or quartered**

**5 ounces leeks, thinly sliced**

**salt and freshly ground black pepper**

**2 tablespoons water**

**8 eggs, beaten with 1/2 teaspoon salt**

**2 tablespoons chopped fresh basil**

**1/4 cup freshly grated Parmesan**

Preheat the broiler.

Heat a large heavy frying pan over high heat. Add the oil and butter and allow the butter to foam. Add the pepper, mushrooms, leeks and a little salt and pepper. Stir the vegetables gently as they cook, and when the pan gets very hot again, add the water. This will stop the vegetables from burning, encourage them to wilt and prevent the need for more oil.

When the vegetables are cooked to your liking, stir the eggs gently into the vegetable mixture. Add the basil and 2 tablespoons of Parmesan. Continue stirring the eggs until they begin to set, then spread the mixture evenly over the pan and sprinkle on the rest of the Parmesan.

Place the pan underneath the hot broiler until the frittata is glazed and slightly puffed.

# Strawberry and Mascarpone Torte

STRAWBERRIES AND CREAM, STRAWBERRY SHORTCAKE, BOTH ARE TRUE BLUE CLASSICS THAT ARE HARD TO BEAT. THIS TORTE STRETCHES THE COMBINATION IDEA A STEP FURTHER: THE LADYFINGERS ADD THE TEXTURE, THE MASCARPONE-EGG MIXTURE IS A DELICATE LAYER OF AIRY FLUFF, AND THE STRAWBERRIES, OF COURSE, SPEAK FOR THEMSELVES! YOU CAN MAKE THE DISH IN INDIVIDUAL MOLDS OR IN ONE SOUFFLÉ DISH. AS THE RECIPE HAS SEVERAL ELEMENTS, IT IS WORTH MAKING THIS QUANTITY. **Serves 6** (V)

**2 pounds fresh strawberries**

**7 tablespoons superfine sugar**

**1 tablespoon lemon juice**

**1 pound mascarpone cheese**

**2/3 cup thick Pastry Cream (see page 180)**

**2 tablespoons Grand Marnier**

**3 eggs, separated**

**6 tablespoons granulated sugar**

**3/4 teaspoon powdered gelatin, softened in 1 tablespoon cold water**

**8 ounces ladyfingers**

Place 3 1/2 cups of the strawberries in a blender or food processor with the superfine sugar and lemon juice. Blend to a smooth purée, then pass through a fine sieve.

Slice the rest of the strawberries into 1/4-inch-thick slices and toss with a spoonful or two of the sauce, just enough to coat the slices.

In a small bowl, beat half the mascarpone with a wooden spoon until soft. Stir in the pastry cream and half the Grand Marnier. Set aside.

Whisk the egg yolks with 3 tablespoons of granulated sugar in a mixing bowl set over a pan of simmering water until the mixture is pale yellow, feels slightly warmer than body temperature and trails off the whisk in ribbons. Whisk the softened gelatin into the egg yolk mixture. Continue to whisk over medium heat until the gelatin has dissolved. Remove from the heat and beat until light and fluffy and the bowl is no longer hot.

Beat the remaining mascarpone with a wooden spoon until soft and fold together with the gelatin-yolk mixture. Fold in the remaining tablespoon of Grand Marnier. Whisk the egg whites with the remaining granulated sugar until the mixture forms soft and glossy peaks, then fold into the egg-mascarpone mixture.

You can assemble the torte in 1 soufflé dish or in six 3-inch soufflé molds or pastry rings. Line the base with ladyfingers and soak them heavily with some of the strawberry sauce. Cover with a single layer of the sliced strawberries. Spoon in a 1/2-inch-thick layer of the pastry cream-mascarpone mixture. Add another layer of ladyfingers but do not soak this layer. It will absorb enough moisture; too much will make the torte lose its shape when unmolded. Cover with another single layer of tossed strawberries. The molds will be just over half full. Fill to the rim with the egg white-mascarpone mixture. Place the tortes in the refrigerator to set for at least 2 hours.

If making in a single soufflé mold, just serve it from the mold after it has been well chilled. If made in the individual molds or rings, the tortes can be unmolded. Run a hot knife around the insides of the soufflé dishes or pastry rings. Carefully tip the tortes out of the dishes or lift off the rings. Smooth out the sides if necessary with a small flexible metal spatula.

To serve, arrange in the center of individual plates and drizzle strawberry sauce around. These tortes can keep only for a day or two in the refrigerator.

CHAPTER EIGHT

# Family Get-Together

To us, a family get-together implies everyone rolling up their sleeves and getting stuck in. The kitchen is the focal point, and the preparation is a social time. For these occasions it's great to cook easy-to-serve items such as soups, roasts and the like. Be sure to make extras, for every family has at least one person who sneaks back in for the leftovers later on in the evening.

## Menu 1

Chicken, Barley and Parsley Broth

Whole-Wheat Bread

Roast Kassler with Cabbage and Potatoes

Chocolate Bread-and-Butter Pudding with Marmalade Sauce

## Menu 2

Salmon Terrine with Sun-Dried Tomato Mayonnaise

Turkey Ossobuco

Risotto with Lemon and Basil

Pumpkin Gingerbread

# Chicken, Barley and Parsley Broth

THIS SOUP HAS BEEN A COMFORT FOOD TO PAUL SINCE HE WAS A WEE LAD. NUTRITIOUS AND EASY TO DIGEST, IT'S A PERFECT REMEDY FOR WHEN ONE FEELS UNDER THE WEATHER. HOWEVER, DON'T WAIT UNTIL YOU HAVE A COLD TO ENJOY IT, AS IT'S DELICIOUS ANY TIME! THE SOUP KEEPS WELL IN THE REFRIGERATOR AND SOME PEOPLE THINK IT TASTES EVEN BETTER THE NEXT DAY. **Serves 6 to 8**

**1 boiling chicken, almost 5 pounds**

**4 quarts water**

**14 ounces onion, finely chopped**

**1 cup polished barley, soaked overnight in water**

**7 ounces carrot, grated (optional)**

**2 tablespoons salt**

**1 tablespoon freshly ground white pepper**

**2 sprigs fresh parsley, finely chopped**

Wash and clean the chicken and place in large pan with the 4 quarts water. Bring to a boil over medium heat and skim off any scum that rises to the surface. Add another 1 1/4 cups cold water (this addition helps release scum) and simmer gently over low heat for about 5 hours, skimming occasionally.

Remove the chicken and let it cool. Add the onion, soaked barley and carrot to the broth and simmer for 30 minutes. When the chicken is cool enough to handle, remove the meat from the carcass. Chop it into bite-size pieces and return it to the broth. Season with salt and pepper to taste. Just before serving the broth, add the chopped parsley.

# Whole-Wheat Bread

WHOLE-WHEAT BREAD IS GREAT. IT HAS TEXTURE, FLAVOR AND SO VERY MANY USES!

**Makes one 2-pound loaf** 

**2 1/3 cups whole-wheat flour, preferably coarse ground**

**1 1/3 cups all-purpose flour**

**3 tablespoons wheat bran**

**1 1/2 teaspoons baking soda**

**pinch of salt**

**1 tablespoon soft brown sugar**

**2 1/2 to 3 cups buttermilk**

Preheat the oven to 400°F. Thoroughly grease a 2-pound loaf pan (9 by 5 by 3 inches).

In a large bowl, stir all the dry ingredients together. Stir in enough buttermilk to form a nice, thick dropping consistency. Pour into the prepared pan and bake in the preheated oven for about 1 1/2 to 2 hours, or until the loaf sounds hollow when tapped on the base. Cool on a wire rack. If you prefer a softer crust, wrap in a slightly dampened cloth and leave to cool.

OVERLEAF:

Family Get-Together, Menu 1

Chicken, Barley and Parsley Broth (page 88)

Whole-Wheat Bread (page 89)

Roast Kassler with Cabbage and Potatoes (page 92)

Chocolate Bread-and-Butter Pudding with Marmalade Sauce (page 93)

Album

TRAFALGAR SQUARE £240
FLEET STREET £220
500
"MONOPOLY"
100

# Roast Kassler
## with Cabbage and Potatoes

THIS IS A SIMPLE ONE-PAN DISH OF HUMBLE ORIGINS, TAKING INSPIRATION FROM THE AGE-OLD CABBAGE AND BACON RECIPES. THE SMOKED GERMAN HAM, KASSLER, PERFUMES THE CABBAGE AND POTATOES WITH ITS RICH SMOKY AROMAS. SUBSTITUTE A SMOKED BACON LOIN IF YOU CAN'T FIND KASSLER. **Serves 6 to 8**

**2 1/4 pounds potatoes, unpeeled and quartered**

**1 head savoy cabbage, about 1 pound, cored and roughly chopped**

**2 1/4 pounds boneless kassler**

**2 tablespoons unsalted butter**

For the sauce:

**2 tablespoons unsalted butter**

**1 tablespoon all-purpose flour**

**2 1/2 cups chicken stock**

**1/4 cup Madeira or port wine**

**1 to 3 tablespoons Dijon mustard**

**salt and freshly ground black pepper**

Preheat the oven to 400°F.

To parboil the potatoes, place them in a large pan, cover with cold salted water and bring to a boil. Simmer for 5 minutes, then drain the potatoes into a colander. This parboiling helps to remove moisture and surface starch from the potatoes, which would make them stick to the roasting pan.

Parboil the cabbage in a large pan of lightly salted water for 2 minutes. Drain it into a colander, refresh in cold water and squeeze the cabbage dry in your hands.

Place the kassler in a large roasting pan and put in the oven. Roast it for about 10 minutes, then add the butter. When the butter has melted, add the potatoes. Roast together for 20 minutes, turning the kassler and potatoes occasionally. Push the potatoes and kassler to one side and add the cabbage. Season the potatoes and cabbage with salt. Roast for a further 10 minutes, turning all the ingredients in the smoky butter.

While the kassler is roasting, make the sauce. Melt the butter in a small pan and add the flour. Cook for 2 minutes, stirring occasionally. Take off the heat and whisk in the cold chicken stock. Whisk until smooth, then return to the heat and simmer for 20 minutes, stirring occasionally.

After a total of 40 minutes, remove the kassler from the oven. Check that the potatoes and cabbage are properly cooked and transfer them to a warmed serving platter. Slice the kassler, arrange on the cabbage and keep warm while you finish the sauce.

Deglaze the juices on the roasting pan with the wine and add to the sauce. Whisk in the mustard and season carefully with salt and pepper. Serve the sauce separately.

# Chocolate Bread-and-Butter Pudding
## with Marmalade Sauce

CHOCOLATE ADDS ANOTHER DIMENSION TO THIS OLD FAVORITE. IF PREFERRED, ONE LARGE BAKING DISH CAN BE USED INSTEAD OF INDIVIDUAL BOWLS. **Serves 6 to 8** (V)

**2 1/4 cups milk**

**2 1/4 cups light cream or half-and-half**

**grated zest of 1 orange**

**1 vanilla bean, split lengthwise**

**1 1/4 cups cocoa powder**

**1/2 loaf unsliced white bread (enough for 6 to 8 slices)**

**8 egg yolks**

**2 eggs**

**1/2 cup superfine sugar**

**7 ounces bittersweet or semisweet chocolate, melted**

**1 1/4 cups chunky-style marmalade**

**1 cup water**

**confectioners' sugar (optional)**

Place the milk, cream, orange zest and the vanilla bean into a pan and bring to a boil. Remove from the heat, whisk in the cocoa and leave to infuse for 30 minutes.

Preheat the oven to 300°F.

Remove the crusts from the bread and cut into 1/4-inch-thick slices. Cut each slice on the diagonal and place two triangles of bread in 6 to 8 individual ramekins.

Whisk together the egg yolks, eggs and sugar until the sugar has dissolved. Strain the milk-cream mixture through a fine sieve onto the eggs and sugar and whisk together. Finally, add the melted chocolate and stir well. Ladle the mixture gently into the ramekins so as not to disturb the bread. Place the ramekins on a baking sheet and fill it with boiling water to come one-third of the way up the sides of the ramekins. Cover this whole bain-marie with plastic wrap and place in the preheated oven for about 40 to 50 minutes. The very center of each pudding should just shake slightly when it is ready. Remove from the oven and remove from the bain-marie.

To make the sauce, place the marmalade and water in a small pan and bring slowly to a boil. Stir and remove from the heat. Cover the top of each pudding with a spoonful or two of the marmalade sauce. Alternatively, serve the marmalade sauce on the side and simply sprinkle a little confectioners' sugar onto each pudding for decoration.

# Salmon Terrine
## with Sun-Dried Tomato Mayonnaise

This is not one of those smooth, textureless terrines that can be very boring and bland. No, this is a beautiful chunky, flavorful specimen that is very versatile. We fed it to the great Californian winemaker Tim Mondavi and his conclusion? "I don't like terrine, but I love this one!" **Serves 8**

**11 ounces leeks, finely chopped**

**2 tablespoons unsalted butter**

**1/4 cup water**

**1/2 teaspoon salt**

For the mousse:

**1 3/4 pounds fresh salmon fillet, skinned and well chilled**

**1 egg, chilled**

**2/3 cup whipping cream, well chilled**

**3/ 4 teaspoon salt**

**1 tablespoon chopped fresh parsley**

**1 tablespoon snipped fresh chives**

**1/4 teaspoon white pepper**

For the sun-dried tomato mayonnaise:

**6 tablespoons mayonnaise**

**1/4 cup Sun-Dried Tomato Vinaigrette (see page 37)**

To garnish:

**a few mixed salad leaves**

**a few fresh chervil leaves**

Preheat the oven to 325°F. Chill the bowl and blade of a food processor for about 15 minutes. Lightly butter a 1-quart terrine dish.

Place a large pan over medium heat and cook the leeks with the butter, water and salt for about 5 minutes, or until the leeks are lightly cooked. Drain into sieve and press with the back of a spoon to remove as much liquid as possible. Allow the leeks to cool.

To make the mousse, check the salmon for errant bones. Roughly chop about 7 ounces of the salmon and cut the remainder in 1/2-inch dice. Purée the chopped salmon with the egg in the food processor until very smooth, cleaning down the sides of the bowl occasionally with a spatula. Add the cream and 1/4 teaspoon of salt and process for 5 seconds. Wipe the sides of the bowl again and process again for 5 seconds. Transfer to a large bowl.

Add the leeks, the diced salmon and all the remaining mousse ingredients. Mix very thoroughly, then place in the prepared terrine, pressing the mixture down well. Cover with a double layer of kitchen foil and stand the terrine in a large baking pan. Fill the pan with 1 1/2 inches of boiling water. Place this bain-marie in the preheated oven and cook for 40 minutes, then remove and allow to cool. Blend together the mayonnaise and vinaigrette.

To serve, slice the terrine and place on cold plates. Garnish with a good dollop of sun-dried tomato mayonnaise and a few salad leaves and sprigs of chervil.

# Turkey Ossobuco

THIS IS AN IDEA THAT PAUL NOTICED IN A COOKERY BOOK YEARS AGO AND, BEING A BIG FAN OF THE FLAVOR OF TURKEY LEG MEAT, HAD ALWAYS MEANT TO TRY. NOW WE CAN'T REMEMBER THE BOOK OR FIND THE RECIPE, SO PAUL HAS DEVELOPED HIS OWN. WE'VE BONED THE TURKEY LEGS, BUT YOU COULD SAW THE LEGS THROUGH THE BONE INTO SECTIONS. THIS DISH REHEATS VERY WELL SO IT CAN BE COOKED TWO DAYS IN ADVANCE, THEN GENTLY REHEATED. **Serves 8**

**3 1/2 pounds boneless, skinless turkey leg meat, cut into 1 1/2-inch cubes**

**3 tablespoons all-purpose flour**

**1/4 cup unsalted butter**

**2 tablespoons oil**

**1 small carrot, diced**

**1 celery stalk, diced**

**1 small onion, diced**

**1 garlic clove, finely chopped**

**1 1/4 cups dry white wine**

**1 bay leaf**

**1/2 teaspoon dried thyme or 1 fresh thyme sprig**

**2 cups meat stock or broth**

**12 ounces fresh plum tomatoes, peeled, seeded and diced, or 1 can (14 ounces) tomatoes, seeded and diced**

**salt and freshly ground black pepper**

Heat a large frying pan over medium-high heat. Roll the turkey meat in the flour. Add the butter and oil to the pan and allow the butter to foam. Add the turkey pieces in one layer and fry until lightly browned on all sides. As they brown, transfer the pieces to a flameproof baking dish or a Dutch oven. Add the diced vegetables and garlic to the frying pan and fry until lightly browned. Add the wine and boil until reduced by half. Tip the wine and vegetables into the baking dish with the remaining ingredients and 1 teaspoon of salt. Bring to a boil, then cover and simmer very gently for 1 1/4 hours (or cook in a preheated oven at 300°F).

When the turkey is cooked and tender, check and season the sauce to taste and strain off any excess fat that has floated to the surface.

# Risotto
## with Lemon and Basil

THIS SIMPLE RISOTTO WAS INSPIRED BY *GREMOLATA*, THE DELICIOUS MIXTURE OF LEMON ZEST, PARSLEY AND GARLIC NORMALLY STREWN OVER OSSOBUCO! THE COMBINATION IS SO DELICIOUS WE DECIDED TO ADD IT TO THE RISOTTO, THEN IT CAN BE SERVED WITH SHELLFISH, CHICKEN OR WHATEVER STRIKES YOUR FANCY.

**Serves 8** 

**1/2 cup plus 2 tablespoons unsalted butter**

**7 ounces onions, chopped**

**2 1/4 cups Arborio or other risotto rice**

**4 cups chicken or vegetable stock, boiling**

**1 garlic clove, finely chopped**

**1 tablespoon grated lemon zest**

**2 tablespoons chopped fresh parsley**

**2 tablespoons chopped fresh basil**

**scant 1 cup grated Parmesan cheese**

Melt 1/4 cup of butter in a large pan over medium heat. Add the onions and fry them gently for 5 minutes, or until they are soft but have no color. Add the rice and allow it to cook with the onions for 2 minutes, stirring well. Add enough boiling stock barely to cover the rice. Stir the rice gently until the stock has been absorbed, then add another ladleful of stock and continue in this way for about 20 minutes, or until the rice is just cooked but has a little bite. There should be enough liquid to make the risotto creamy. Now add the remaining ingredients and stir until all the butter has been absorbed. Serve at once.

# Pumpkin Gingerbread

WE FIND THAT THE SWEET, SUCCULENT FLAVOR OF PUMPKIN TENDS NOT TO BE APPRECIATED IN IRELAND. BUT IF YOU TRY THIS GINGERBREAD, YOU'LL SEE HOW IT ADDS DEPTH, MOISTNESS AND A NATURAL-TASTING SWEETNESS. THE SPICES HERE COMPLEMENT ITS DELICATE FLAVOR. IF YOU WANT TO USE FRESH PUMPKIN, SIMPLY HALVE OR QUARTER THE PUMPKIN AND SCOOP OUT THE SEEDS. PLACE THE PIECES ON A BAKING SHEET AND BAKE FOR ABOUT 1 HOUR AT 325°F. REMOVE FROM THE OVEN, SCRAPE ALL THE FLESH FREE AND PASS IT THROUGH A FINE SIEVE OR THROUGH A FOOD MILL. **Serves 8** (V)

**1 3/4 cups all-purpose flour**

**pinch of salt**

**1 teaspoon baking soda**

**2 teaspoons ground ginger**

**1/2 teaspoon ground cinnamon**

**1/2 teaspoon ground cloves**

**1/2 teaspoon ground allspice**

**1/2 cup boiling water**

**1/2 cup molasses**

**1/2 cup pumpkin purée (fresh or canned)**

**3/4 cup granulated sugar**

**5 tablespoons unsalted butter, softened**

**1 egg**

**2 1/2 cups Vanilla Custard Sauce (see page 181) made with 1 cinnamon stick or 1 teaspoon ground cinnamon**

Preheat the oven to 350°F. Grease a 9-inch cake pan.

Sift together all the dry ingredients except the sugar. Mix together the boiling water and molasses. After it has cooled slightly, stir in the pumpkin purée.

Cream together the sugar and butter until light. Slowly mix in the egg and beat again until fully incorporated. Alternately fold in the dry ingredients and molasses mixture and mix thoroughly. Pour into the prepared cake pan and bake in the preheated oven for about 35 minutes, or until a skewer inserted in the center comes out clean. Remove from the oven and cool on a wire rack.

To make the custard, follow the custard recipe on page 181 but let the cinnamon infuse with the scalded milk for at least 30 minutes before making the custard.

To serve, slice the cake into wedges and serve each portion on a plate with a generous amount of cinnamon custard poured over the top.

CHAPTER NINE

# Cream of the Crop

Here, as the title suggests, we're talking about the best of the best. The ingredients given in these recipes may not always be in plentiful supply, but it's worth searching out these treasured and sometimes mysterious items. We've kept this chapter vegetarian because we feel that it reflects today's trends and demands.

### Menu 1

Wild Mushroom and Artichoke Tartlets

Spaghetti with Baby Vegetables and Basil

Summer Pudding

### Menu 2

Californian Roast Tomato and Bell Pepper Soup

Warm Goat Cheese with Grilled Vegetables

Olive and Herb Bread

Lemon Curd with Fresh Strawberries

# Wild Mushroom and Artichoke Tartlets

FROM THE POINT OF VIEW OF THE PROFESSIONAL CHEF, THERE ARE FEW VEGETABLES TO COMPARE WITH ARTICHOKES OR THE ELUSIVE WILD MUSHROOM. BOTH ARE WORTH GETTING TO KNOW, SO TRY THIS RECIPE WITH SHIITAKE OR OYSTER MUSHROOMS AND SOME ARTICHOKE HEARTS, AND YOU'LL BE WELL ON YOUR WAY. INSTEAD OF FRESH ARTICHOKES, YOU COULD USE A JAR OR CAN OF GOOD-QUALITY ARTICHOKES.

**Serves 4** 

**8 ounces Savory Pastry (see page 177)**

**7 ounces flavorful wild or cultivated mushrooms such as chanterelles, porcini, shiitakes or oyster mushrooms**

**2 tablespoons light olive oil**

**2 tablespoons unsalted butter**

**salt and freshly ground black pepper**

**2 large artichokes or 1 can (11 ounces) prepared artichoke hearts**

**juice of 1/2 lemon**

**1/4 garlic clove, crushed**

**1 tablespoon chopped fresh parsley**

For the sauce:

**7 tablespoons whipping cream**

**1/2 cup unsalted butter, chilled and diced**

**1 tablespoon lemon juice**

**1 tablespoon snipped fresh chives**

**1 tablespoon chopped fresh parsley**

Grease four 4-inch tartlet pans. Roll out the pastry to about 1/8 inch thick and use to line the prepared tartlet pans. Chill for at least 30 minutes.

Preheat the oven to 400°F.

Cover the pastry with parchment paper, fill with pie weights and bake in the preheated oven for 10 to 15 minutes, or until cooked and light brown. Remove the weights and the paper. Set aside.

Prepare the mushrooms, cleaning, cutting and trimming them as necessary. Heat a large frying pan over high heat, add 1 tablespoon each of oil and butter and add the mushrooms and a little salt and pepper. Fry for about 3 to 4 minutes, or until the mushrooms are cooked. Keep warm.

As you prepare the artichokes, keep them in a bowl of water with a little lemon juice to prevent them from discoloring; it makes no real difference to the flavour. Carefully trim all the outside leaves with a sharp knife until you are left with only the heart. Cut out the hairy choke in the center of each heart and cut each heart into quarters. You should now have 8 triangle-shaped pieces of artichoke heart; cut each one into 3 slivers.

To cook, heat a frying pan over medium heat. Add the remaining butter and oil, the artichokes and a little salt and pepper. Cook over low heat for about 10 minutes, or until the artichoke slivers are soft and beginning to brown. If you are using canned artichokes, simply drain, cut into manageable pieces and panfry over high heat until light brown. Add the mushrooms, garlic and parsley to the artichokes. Mix together and keep warm while you make the sauce.

To make the sauce, bring the cream to a boil in a small pan, then whisk in the butter and add the lemon juice, herbs, and salt and pepper to taste. Keep warm but do not boil.

To serve, fill each tartlet shell with the artichoke-mushroom mixture. Present on warmed plates surrounded with a little sauce.

# Spaghetti
## with Baby Vegetables and Basil

We've included this recipe here for two reasons. Firstly because we eat it all the time at home, and secondly to demonstrate the importance of good-quality ingredients. Here we see simple spaghetti transformed to world-class gourmet fodder by the addition of delicate, tender vegetables bursting with seasonal freshness. So when you're shopping for this recipe, leave your list at home and buy whatever looks good and fresh. **Serves 4 to 6** (V)

**1 1/4 pounds spaghetti**
**1 tablespoon vegetable oil**
**1/4 cup unsalted butter**
**2 ounces mushrooms, quartered**
**2 small zucchini, cut into rounds**
**6 red cherry tomatoes, halved**
**6 yellow cherry tomatoes, halved**
**6 baby leeks, split**
**7 ounces broccoli florets, cut to thumbnail size**
**6 asparagus spears, cut into 2-inch lengths**
**6 green onions**
**1/3 cup shelled fresh green peas**
**2 ounces snow peas or sugar snap peas**
**2 cups fresh basil leaves, chopped**
**1 garlic clove, crushed and chopped**
**2 tablespoons virgin olive oil**
**salt and freshly ground black pepper**
**3/4 cup grated Parmesan cheese**

Fill each of 2 large pans with about 6 quarts of lightly salted water and bring to a boil. Add the spaghetti to one pan and boil for about 10 to 15 minutes, or until al dente. Meanwhile, heat a large frying pan over medium heat. Add the oil and half the butter. When the butter is foaming, add the mushrooms and zucchini and cook for about 4 minutes, or until lightly browned and tender. Remove from the heat and add the cherry tomatoes.

While the mushrooms and zucchini are cooking, drop the remaining vegetables into the other pan, starting with vegetables that require more cooking such as leeks and broccoli. A minute later, add the asparagus and green onions, then after another minute add all the peas and cook for a further 3 minutes. Drain, add to the other vegetables and keep warm.

Drain the spaghetti, then transfer it back into a warm pan. Add the basil, garlic, olive oil, remaining butter and the vegetables. Toss the spaghetti gently with the vegetables. Season with salt and pepper. Serve piping hot with the Parmesan cheese on the side.

# Summer Pudding

When it's berry season, it's time for Summer Pudding. Use what is available to you: strawberries can be substituted, loganberries or blackberries as well, as long as there's still about 3 ounces of red currants the pudding will set. What could be better? **Serves 4** (V)

**1/2 loaf white bread, sliced**

**1 pint (2 cups) fresh blackberries, hulled**

**1 pint (2 cups) fresh raspberries**

**5 ounces (1 1/4 cups) fresh red currants**

**2/3 cup superfine sugar**

**fresh mint sprigs to decorate**

**clotted or whipped cream or vanilla ice cream to serve (optional)**

Trim all the crusts off the bread, and use most of it to line a 2 1/2-cup glass bowl, covering the base and sides completely.

Place all the berries and sugar in a pan and bring to a boil. Simmer for about 3 minutes, then remove from the heat. Leave to cool slightly.

Ladle the berries into the bread-lined bowl, filling to just 1/4 inch below the top, reserving any leftover juice. Cover with more bread slices and cover with a plate that fits just inside the rim of the bowl. Place a weight to help compress the berries. Chill the pudding and any leftover juice in the refrigerator overnight.

The next day, turn the pudding out by inverting onto a rimmed plate. Pour the reserved juice over any parts of the bread that didn't take as much color. Decorate with mint.

To serve, cut individual portions and serve with clotted cream, whipped cream or even vanilla ice cream.

# Californian Roast Tomato and Bell Pepper Soup

WHEN WE LIVED IN CALIFORNIA THIS WAS ONE OF THE MOST POPULAR SOUPS AROUND. PAUL LEARNED IT FROM A CHEF WHO HAD PICKED IT UP WHILE WORKING IN THE FAMOUS SAN FRANCISCO BAY AREA RESTAURANT CHEZ PANISSE. IT'S A SIMPLE SOUP: EVERYTHING GOES INTO A BAKING PAN AND THEN INTO THE OVEN UNTIL TENDER, THEN IT IS PURÉED—AND THAT'S IT. **Serves 6** (V)

**3 1/4 pounds very ripe tomatoes, halved**

**2 red bell peppers, seeded and roughly chopped**

**2 large onions, roughly chopped**

**6 garlic cloves, crushed**

**3 tablespoons tomato paste**

**3 tablespoons olive oil**

**salt and freshly ground black pepper**

**1 teaspoon fresh thyme leaves**

**2 tablespoons fresh basil leaves**

**1 tablespoon fresh parsley leaves**

**water or stock**

**sugar**

To garnish:

**6 fresh flat-leaf parsley sprigs**

**6 tablespoons whipping cream**

Preheat the oven to 400°F.

In a fairly deep baking pan, mix together the vegetables, garlic, tomato paste, olive oil and 1 teaspoon of salt. Bake in the preheated oven for 1 hour, stirring occasionally. The skins of the tomatoes and peppers should blacken slightly.

Remove from the oven and purée the soup in a blender or food processor, then pass through a sieve, in batches if necessary. Put the herb leaves in the blender or food processor with a few ladles of the soup and purée for about 15 seconds. Stir it back into the soup. Correct the consistency of the soup by adding a little water or stock. Check and adjust the seasoning with salt, pepper and sugar to taste. Reheat gently if necessary.

Serve the soup with a sprig of parsley and a tablespoon of cream in each bowl.

# Warm Goat Cheese
## with Grilled Vegetables

WARM, GRILLED GOAT CHEESE IS ONE OF LIFE'S SIMPLE PLEASURES. SOME SAY THAT IT IS AN ACQUIRED TASTE, BUT WE BELIEVE THEY'RE TALKING ABOUT SOMETHING OLD AND STALE, NOT THE BEAUTIFUL, TENDER, AROMATIC FRESH CHEESES THAT WE LOVE. THEY SEEM TO LEND THEMSELVES TO ANY VEGETABLE DISH, MAKING SUPERB FIRST COURSES OR SATISFYING LUNCHES. AND DON'T ALWAYS LOOK FOR A FRENCH GOAT CHEESE; ASK YOUR CHEESE SHOP FOR LOCALLY PRODUCED ONES. THEY'RE OFTEN JUST AS GOOD. **Serves 6** (V)

**1 log fresh goat cheese, 1 1/4 pounds**

**2 tablespoons butter, softened**

**a selection of grilled vegetables (see page 110)**

**6 tablespoons chili oil**

**cracked black pepper**

Preheat the broiler.

To cut the cheese neatly, take a mug of boiling water and a thin-bladed knife. Dip the knife into the water, then cut a section of cheese. Repeat until you have 6 neat sections. Place the cheese flat on a broiler pan and spread each generously with butter. This helps the cheese brown nicely as it cooks. Broil for about 2 to 3 minutes, or until the cheese slices are nicely browned and warmed through. With a large spatula transfer them to warmed plates. If the cheese has a rind, remove it at this stage. It should simply pull off.

Surround each cheese with a selection of grilled vegetables, a little chili oil and some cracked black pepper.

# Olive and Herb Bread

THESE LITTLE ROUNDS OF BREAD ARE CHEWY AND TASTY, THE PERFECT ACCOMPANIMENT TO MANY A SOUP, SALAD OR STARTER. OF COURSE, ALTERNATIVE HERBS SUCH AS THYME OR BASIL CAN BE SUBSTITUTED; OR TRY SUN-DRIED TOMATOES INSTEAD OF OLIVES. THE BREAD ROUNDS FREEZE VERY WELL WHEN WRAPPED IN PLASTIC WRAP AND ARE HANDY TO HAVE AS STANDBYS. **Makes four to six 6-inch rounds** 

**1 tablespoon active dry yeast**

**2 cups plus 2 tablespoons water**

**5 2/3 cups bread flour**

**1 1/2 tablespoons salt**

**2 tablespoons olive oil**

**3 tablespoons finely chopped black olives**

**1 tablespoon finely chopped fresh parsley**

**1 tablespoon finely chopped fresh rosemary**

Dissolve the yeast in 3/4 cup of the warm water and leave for 5 minutes, or until foamy. Place the flour and salt in a stand mixer. Add the yeast mixture with the remaining water and the olive oil. Mix with a dough hook for several minutes until a workable dough forms. Toss in the chopped olives and herbs and mix again until the dough is shiny, elastic and smooth. Place in a greased bowl, cover with plastic wrap and leave to rise for about 1 1/2 hours, or until doubled in bulk.

Tip the risen dough on to a lightly floured surface and divide into 4 to 6 even portions. Taking one piece at a time, roll the dough into a ball, then roll the dough out into a 6-inch round about 1 inch thick.

Take a razor blade or very sharp knife and score each round with about five parallel slashes, cutting right through the dough, leaving a perimeter of unslashed dough of about 1 inch around the outside. Place these rounds on a floured baking sheet, cover loosely with plastic wrap and leave to rise for about 30 minutes, or until doubled in size.

Preheat the oven to 400°F.

Bake the loaves in the preheated oven for 25 to 30 minutes, or until browned. Remove from the oven and cool on a wire rack.

OVERLEAF:

Cream of the Crop, Menu 2

Californian Roast Tomato and Bell Pepper Soup (page 103)

Warm Goat Cheese with Grilled Vegetables (page 104)

Olive and Herb Bread (page 105)

Lemon Curd with Fresh Strawberries (page 108)

# Lemon Curd
## with Fresh Strawberries

LEMON AND STRAWBERRIES ARE SIMPLY GLORIOUS TOGETHER, BUT THIS DISH CAN EASILY BE SERVED WITH ANY OTHER BERRY OR SUMMER FRUITS SUCH AS PEACHES OR FRESH APRICOTS. YOU COULD EVEN TRY USING LIME INSTEAD OF LEMON, AND SERVE IT WITH PAPAYA OR MANGO. IF YOU LIKE A REALLY LIGHT MIXTURE, YOU CAN INCREASE THE AMOUNT OF CREAM—EVEN DOUBLE IT—BUT THIS AMOUNT GIVES A WONDERFUL TEXTURE AND TAKES THE HEAVINESS OUT OF THE CURD. **Serves 6** (V)

**2 eggs**

**2 egg yolks**

**2/3 cup superfine sugar**

**grated zest of 1 or 2 lemons**

**juice of 2 lemons (about 6 tablespoons)**

**1 1/2 cups plus 1 tablespoon unsalted butter, chilled and diced**

**1 cup whipping cream**

**1 pint (2 cups) fresh strawberries**

Place the eggs, egg yolks and sugar in a heavy-based pan and whisk briskly to combine well. Add the zest and juice of the lemons, whisking again. Add the diced butter, place over medium heat and cook, stirring continuously, for about 3 minutes without allowing the mixture to boil. If using a thermometer, the curd is ready at 325°F. Remove from the heat.

Transfer the mixture to a plastic container (it should have an airtight lid) and cover with plastic wrap immediately. Press the plastic wrap right against the curd and poke a slit or two with a knife to let the steam out. This will prevent a skin from forming. Leave the mixture to cool; it will thicken during the cooling period.

Whip the cream until it holds soft peaks, then fold it into the cooled mixture. Cover with the airtight lid and chill in the rerfrigerator. It will keep for about 5 days.

To serve, hull and halve the strawberries. Place a dollop of curd in the center of each bowl and generously scatter strawberries all around the curd.

CHAPTER TEN

# Salad Magic

Salads are great—healthy, easy to prepare and delicious! Is it any wonder that they are gaining so much in popularity? Whatever you do, don't be bound by the conventional lettuce. There's a whole world of salad products and condiments available, as well as, of course, your own creativity.

### Menu 1

Warm Salad of Grilled Vegetables

Chicken Paillard on a Watercress Salad with Mustard Butter

Exotic Fruit Salad in Lime-Ginger Syrup

### Menu 2

Tomato and Mozzarella Salad with Basil Oil

Seared Beef Salad with Blue Cheese Dressing

Winter Soup of Poached Pears and Sun-Dried Cherries with Amaretto Custard

# Warm Salad of Grilled Vegetables

This is a salad that we often cook on the barbecue at the restaurant. Here we've adopted the technique for the home kitchen to create a meal in itself. **Serves 4 to 6** (V)

**1 red bell pepper**

**1 yellow bell pepper**

**7 tablespoons light olive oil**

**1 zucchini**

**1 eggplant**

**1 red onion**

**1 artichoke heart, choke removed**

**3 small leeks, split**

**6 large mushrooms**

**salt and freshly ground black pepper**

**a selection of salad leaves**

**7 tablespoons virgin olive oil**

**1/4 cup balsamic vinegar**

**4 ounces Parmesan cheese, shaved with a peeler**

**1 tablespoon chopped fresh thyme**

**1 tablespoon chopped fresh parsley**

**1 tablespoon black peppercorns, cracked**

To prepare the vegetables, rub the peppers with a little light olive oil and roast them under a very hot broiler or in a very hot oven until the skins are blackening. Peel, seed and slice each one into 6 pieces. Slice the zucchini and eggplant into 1/2-inch-thick slices and drizzle lightly with light olive oil. Cut the onion and the artichoke heart into 6 wedges. Blanch the onion wedges and the leeks in a pan of boiling salted water for 2 minutes each, then drain and refresh them under cold water.

Preheat the broiler. Arrange all the vegetables separately on broiler pans and brush lightly with light olive oil. Season with salt and pepper. Grill each vegetable separately until just cooked. The peppers, leeks and the artichoke only need 1 to 2 minutes, while the mushrooms, onion, zucchini and eggplant will take about 5 minutes each.

To serve, arrange the vegetables attractively on the plates and place a few mixed salad leaves in the center of each arrangement. Drizzle with the virgin olive oil and the balsamic vinegar. Sprinkle with the Parmesan, herbs and black pepper.

# Chicken Paillard on a Watercress Salad
## with Mustard Butter

THIS IS ESSENTIALLY A MAIN COURSE LUNCH SALAD, ALTHOUGH IT WOULD WORK WELL AS A STARTER, TOO. THE DELICIOUS SAUCE IS FORMED AS THE BUTTER MELTS AND COMBINES WITH THE JUICES OF THE CHICKEN.

**Serves 4**

**2 tablespoons butter**

**2 tablespoons light vegetable oil**

**2 1/2 cups diced cooked, peeled potato (3/4-inch dice)**

**4 skinless chicken breasts, 6 ounces each**

**2 bunches watercress**

For the mustard butter:

**1/2 cup unsalted butter, softened**

**1 to 2 tablespoons whole-grain mustard**

**few drops fresh lemon juice**

**salt and freshly ground white pepper**

Preheat the broiler or barbecue.

To prepare the mustard butter, beat the softened butter with 1 tablespoon of mustard in a small bowl. Taste the butter and add more mustard if desired. Add the lemon juice and season to taste with salt and pepper. Set aside.

In a large heavy frying pan, heat half the butter and oil until it begins to color. Sauté the potatoes until light golden and slightly crispy. Season with salt and pepper and keep warm while preparing the chicken.

Lay the chicken fillets on a cutting board. Cut into the more curved side of each, almost to the other side. Open the fillets like a book and press each one flat. Season generously with salt and pepper, brush each one with a little oil and butter and place on the highest rack under the broiler. Cook for 5 minutes on the first side, then turn over and cook for just 1 minute more. While these are cooking, prepare the watercress by picking over and washing as necessary. Dry in a salad spinner.

To serve, arrange the watercress attractively on each plate and sprinkle the sautéed potato around. Place the paillard with the nicely brown side upward in the center and top with a spoonful of the mustard butter.

# Exotic Fruit Salad
## in Lime-Ginger Syrup

A fruit salad is always a pleasing way to end a meal, and an exotic one such as this can be sublime. It can be served on its own for a light ending to a meal, or you could offer it with a fruit sorbet or coconut ice cream. Make sure you choose ripe, unblemished fruits that are ready for eating. The syrup only accentuates the flavors that are there. It can't add flavor to fruit that is tasteless or underripe. If you have star fruit, some strawberries or even a can of lichees, you can add them to the salad. Whatever fruits you are using, give a thought to color and shape as you are preparing them. You can store the syrup in the refrigerator and use it again and again, so make this quantity of syrup and just prepare enough fruit to suit the number you are serving. Always strain the syrup through a fine sieve before storing. **Serves 6 to 8** (V)

For the syrup:

**1 1/4 cups sugar**

**1 3/4 cups water**

**1 1/2 ounces fresh ginger, peeled and sliced**

**zest of 2 limes, in large strips**

**5 tablespoons good-quality honey**

For the salad:

**1 medium pineapple**

**1 ripe mango**

**1 ripe papaya**

**2 kiwifruits**

**candied lime zest to garnish (optional)**

To make the syrup, place the sugar and 1/4 cup of water in a heavy-based pan and heat gently, stirring occasionally, until the sugar has dissolved. Raise the heat to high and cook, without stirring, until golden caramel. Brush down the sides of the pan with a pastry brush dipped in water a couple of times as it is boiling. This helps reduce the chance of the caramel crystallizing. Remove from the heat and slowly add the rest of the water. Be careful as this may spit and splatter. Return to low heat just until all the caramel has dissolved. Take off the heat and add the ginger, lime zest and honey. Set aside to infuse for at least 30 minutes.

Meanwhile, prepare the various exotic fruits. Peel and core the pineapple, and slice into attractive pieces. Do the same with the mango. Peel and seed the papaya and peel the kiwifruits before slicing or cutting up. Place all the fruit in a bowl.

About 10 minutes before serving, strain the syrup through a fine sieve and pour it over the fruit. If using more delicate items such as strawberries, only marinate them for 1 to 2 minutes, as they will start to go very mushy if left too long.

To serve, ladle individual portions of the exotic fruits into glass bowls with enough of the syrup. Decorate with candied lime zest if desired.

# Tomato and Mozzarella Salad
## with Basil Oil

It may seem a little odd having a tomato and mozzarella salad in an Irish cookbook. But we do have the tomatoes and the basil, and we occasionally get a superb English mozzarella from Neals Yard in London. This is a salad that is hugely enjoyed at the restaurant. Reserve the remaining basil oil for salads or pasta. **Serves 4** (V)

**2 or 3 ripe red tomatoes**

**2 or 3 ripe yellow tomatoes**

**14 ounces fresh mozzarella cheese in water**

**salt and cracked black pepper**

**6 large fresh basil leaves, finely shredded**

For the basil oil (makes scant 1 cup):

**3 cups fresh basil leaves**

**3/4 cup olive oil**

**1 garlic clove, crushed**

**1/4 teaspoon salt**

Blanch the tomatoes by placing them in boiling water for 12 seconds. Refresh immediately under cold water. This process loosens the skin, and they should peel very easily. Cut each tomato in half, and then each half into quarters. Drain the mozzarella. Cut the mozzarella in the same way as the tomatoes so that you have pieces that are a similar size and shape. Season the tomatoes lightly with salt. Arrange the tomato and mozzarella pieces on large plates in almost a checkerboard fashion but leaving spaces between the pieces.

To make the basil oil, simply process all the ingredients together in a blender or food processor or a mortar until you have a fairly smooth mixture.

To finish each plate, drip a little of the basil oil from a spoon into the spaces left between the tomatoes and cheese so that you have a beautiful contrast of colors. Sprinkle each plate with some cracked black pepper and shredded basil.

OVERLEAF:
Salad Magic, Menu 2
Tomato and Mozzarella Salad with Basil Oil (page 113)
Seared Beef Salad with Blue Cheese Dressing (page 116)
Winter Soup of Poached Pears and Sun-Dried Cherries with Amaretto Custard (page 117)

# Seared Beef Salad
## with Blue Cheese Dressing

In our opinion beef and blue cheese go together famously. The right touch is required, though, and the searing of the beef in this recipe lightens its flavor so that it stands up to the cheese. This would make a great quick lunch or a buffet dish, as everything can be prepared even a day ahead and then assembled at the last minute. **Serves 4**

**12 ounces beef fillet, trimmed and in one piece**

**1 tablespoon olive oil**

**1/2 teaspoon salt**

**2 teaspoons black peppercorns, cracked**

For the celery:

**3 celery stalks, sliced on the diagonal 1/2 inch thick**

**2/3 cup water**

**3 tablespoons olive oil**

**1/4 teaspoon salt**

**1/2 teaspoon black peppercorns, cracked**

For the dressing:

**2 ounces blue cheese, such as Cashel Blue, Stilton, or Roquefort, crumbled**

**2/3 cup Standard Vinaigrette (see page 178)**

To serve and garnish:

**mixed salad leaves**

**1 tablespoon snipped fresh chives**

**a few fresh chervil leaves**

Make sure that the beef fillet is trimmed and free of sinew and fat. Cut it in half lengthwise so that you have two longish, flat pieces. Season these with olive oil, salt and pepper.

Heat a cast-iron frying pan over high heat until very hot. Add the beef and cook for 2 minutes on each side for rare or 5 minutes for medium well. This is quite a smoky process, but the final result makes it worthwhile. When cooked, transfer the beef to a plate and allow to cool.

To cook the celery, place it in a small pan with the other ingredients. Cover tightly with foil and simmer for 4 minutes. Remove the pan from the heat and allow the celery to cook in the liquid.

To make the dressing, simply whisk the crumbled cheese with the vinaigrette in a small bowl.

To serve, slice the beef into about 12 slices. Arrange the beef slices on cold plates with a little celery between them. Place the salad leaves in the center and spoon on a little dressing. Finish with the snipped chives and a few chervil leaves.

# Winter Soup
## of Poached Pears and Sun-Dried Cherries with Amaretto Custard

WARM SOUPS OF CUSTARD AND FRUIT MAY NOT SPRING TO MIND IMMEDIATELY FOR MOST PEOPLE AS A DESSERT OPTION, BUT ONCE TRIED, THEY ARE FOREVER APPRECIATED. YOU CAN USE CANNED PEARS IF YOU DON'T HAVE TIME TO POACH FRESH FRUIT (SEE PAGE 80). YOU'LL FIND THAT THE SUN-DRIED CHERRIES ARE AVAILABLE IN MOST DELICATESSENS, BUT IF YOU CAN'T FIND THEM, TRY GOLDEN RAISINS OR DRIED BLUEBERRIES. ONE OR TWO AMARETTI WOULD BE A GREAT ACCOMPANIMENT TO SERVE WITH THIS, BUT THEY AREN'T ESSENTIAL. THEY ARE ITALIAN COOKIES WITH A BITTER ALMOND FLAVOR AND ARE AVAILABLE IN MOST LARGE SUPERMARKETS OR DELICATESSENS. **Serves 4** (V)

**2 1/8 cups milk**

**1/2 vanilla bean, split lengthwise, or 1/2 teaspoon vanilla extract**

**3/4 cup ground almonds**

**6 egg yolks**

**2/3 cup superfine sugar**

**1/4 cup amaretto liqueur**

**4 poached pears (see page 80, omitting the wine)**

**1/2 cup pitted sun-dried cherries, soaked in boiling water until cooled**

**1/3 cup sliced almonds, toasted**

**amaretti to serve (optional)**

Place the milk, vanilla bean (if using vanilla extract, add later) and ground almonds in a pan over medium to high heat and bring to a boil. Remove from the heat and leave to infuse for about 20 minutes.

Whisk the egg yolks and sugar together in a bowl until lightened in color and the sugar has dissolved. Whisking continuously, slowly pour the milk into the yolk-sugar mixture and whisk together. Pour this mixture back into the pan and stir over low heat until the mixture has thickened enough to coat the back of the spoon and will hold if you run your finger along the middle of the back of the spoon. When it has reached the desired thickness, strain the custard through a fine sieve. Remove the vanilla bean, if used, and scrape the seeds into the custard. Stir in the liqueur. (Add the vanilla extract at this point, if using.) Place the custard in a heated thermos to keep it nice and warm for serving.

Lay the poached pears on a baking sheet lined with paper towels to drain off the excess liquid. Halve, core and slice the pears into fine wedges or slices.

To serve, arrange the pear slices and plumped up cherries in soup plates and pour the warm amaretto custard sauce over and around them. Decorate with a sprinkle of toasted sliced almonds and, if desired, some amaretti on the side.

CHAPTER ELEVEN

# Dinner for 2 on a Budget

We all at one time or another have occasions when it is necessary to count every penny and work out the cost of everything. But don't take it as a disaster. Instead, look at it as a chance to be creative. Good food doesn't always have to be expensive. With a little thought, and perhaps a little more labor, it's possible to come up with some menus that are real winners.

## Menu 1

Crispy Fried Cod with Lentils and Vinegar

Breast of Turkey with Leeks, Mushrooms and Sliced Potatoes

Stuffed Baked Pear

## Menu 2

Tomato Salad with Shallots, Balsamic Vinegar and Thyme

Skate with Chili and Basil Cream

Spiced Roast Cabbage

Peach Crumble with Raspberry Cream

# Crispy Fried Cod
## with Lentils and Vinegar

THIS RECIPE TAKES ITS INSPIRATION FROM DEEP-FRIED COD AND MUSHY PEAS. THIS VERSION IS VERY MUCH LIGHTER AND PRETTIER BUT HAS ALL THE FLAVORS. **Serves 2**

**2 cod fillets, 4 ounces each**
**1/4 cup whipping cream**
**1 egg white**
**vegetable oil for deep-frying**
**1 teaspoon chopped fresh parsley**

For the lentils:

**1/4 cup French Puy lentils or other small lentils**
**1 1/2 cups stock**
**1/2 teaspoon salt**
**1 tablespoon finely diced onion**
**1 tablespoon finely diced carrot**
**1 tablespoon finely diced leek**
**1 tablespoon finely diced celery**
**1 tablespoon finely diced potato**
**3 tablespoons sherry vinegar**
**1/4 cup unsalted butter, chilled and diced**

For the spiced flour:

**1/4 cup all-purpose flour**
**2 teaspoons baking powder**
**1/2 teaspoon cayenne pepper**
**1/2 teaspoon ground thyme**
**1/2 teaspoon white pepper**
**1/2 teaspoon garlic powder**
**1/2 teaspoon salt**

To cook the lentils, first rinse in plenty of cold water, then put into a small pan with the stock and salt. Bring to a boil and simmer for 10 minutes. Add the diced vegetables and cook for a further 10 to 15 minutes, or until the vegetables and lentils are fully cooked. Add the sherry vinegar and whisk in the diced butter. Keep warm until needed. If you need to plan ahead, the lentils can be cooked a day or two in advance and kept in the refrigerator. If you're doing this, don't add the butter until just before serving.

Preheat a deep-fat fryer or a large pan of oil to 375°F, or until a cube of bread browns in about 40 seconds.

Sift together the ingredients for the spiced flour. In a small bowl, mix the cream with the egg white. Dredge the cod fillets in the spiced flour. "Massage" the fish in the cream mixture, then back again into the flour. Repeat again if you prefer a slightly thicker crust. Carefully drop the cod into the hot oil and cook for about 4 minutes, or until each fillet is crisp and golden. Drain on paper towels.

To serve, spoon a generous amount of lentils onto warmed serving plates and top with the cod and a sprinkling of parsley to garnish.

# Breast of Turkey

## with Leeks, Mushrooms and Sliced Potatoes

THIS DISH IS A FAR CRY FROM THE TURKEY RECIPES THAT NEED TO BE STARTED OFF IN THE MIDDLE OF THE NIGHT IN ORDER TO BE READY FOR LUNCH. YOUNG TURKEY BREASTS DON'T NEED A LONG COOKING TIME; IN FACT, THEY CAN BE TREATED BASICALLY THE SAME AS CHICKEN. **Serves 2**

**1 turkey breast, about 1 pound**

**salt and freshly ground black pepper**

**3 tablespoons vegetable oil**

**1/2 cup plus 2 tablespoons unsalted butter, chilled and diced**

**4 ounces mushrooms, quartered**

**4 ounces leeks, sliced 1/2 inch thick**

**4 to 6 baby potatoes, parboiled then sliced**

**1 tablespoon finely chopped shallot**

**3 tablespoons dry white wine**

**1/4 cup water**

**1/4 teaspoon chopped fresh rosemary**

Preheat the oven to 400°F.

Trim the turkey breast, removing any excess fat. Season generously with salt and pepper. Heat an ovenproof frying pan over medium heat. When hot, add 1 tablespoon of oil and 1 tablespoon of butter. Allow the butter to foam, then add the turkey breast skin-side down and cook for about 2 to 3 minutes, or until the skin is nicely colored. Turn over for 1 minute to seal the other side. Turn back onto the skin side and place in the oven for 20 minutes, or until firm to the touch.

While the turkey is roasting, cook the vegetables. Panfry the mushrooms over high heat in 2 tablespoons of butter with a little salt and pepper. In another pan fry the sliced potatoes with 2 tablespoons of oil and 1 tablespoon of butter until golden brown. Cook the leeks in another pan with 1 tablespoon of butter, a good splash of water and a little salt and pepper for about 3 minutes, or until the water has evaporated and the leeks are tender. Keep all the vegetables warm.

Remove the turkey from the oven and allow to rest for 5 minutes in a warm place.

To make the sauce, tip out any oil from the turkey pan. Add the shallot to the pan over gentle heat and cook for 2 minutes. Stir in the wine, scraping the bottom of the pan to loosen all the caramelized juices. Boil until almost all the wine has evaporated, then add the water and bring to a boil again. Add the rosemary, then dice the remaining butter and whisk.

To serve, spoon the vegetables attractively around the outside of warmed plates. Slice the turkey breast and fan the slices in the center. Top with a little sauce and serve.

OVERLEAF:

Dinner for 2 on a Budget, Menu 1

Crispy Fried Cod with Lentils and Vinegar (page 119)

Breast of Turkey with Leeks, Mushrooms and Sliced Potatoes (page 120)

Stuffed Baked Pear (page 124)

Cod / Cream.
Turkey
Leek &
Mush
£9.33

# Stuffed Baked Pear

THE SWEET, PLEASANT TASTE OF A GOOD EATING PEAR NEEDS LITTLE ADORNMENT. THIS SIMPLE FILLING OF ALMOND AND GINGER OFFERS A COMPLEMENTARY ALLIANCE OF FLAVORS. WE SERVE IT WITH YOGURT, BUT AN ICE CREAM WOULD SUIT IT JUST AS WELL. A TIP TO REMEMBER: IF THE PEAR IS VERY ROUNDED AND WILL NOT LAY EASILY IN A HORIZONTAL POSITION, SLICE A LITTLE BIT OFF THE ROUND BEFORE STUFFING IT, TO GIVE A LITTLE FLAT BASE ON WHICH TO STAND. THE PASTE STORES WELL IN THE REFRIGERATOR, SO WE HAVE GIVEN A QUANTITY THAT WILL SERVE UP TO SIX. **Serves 2** (V)

**1 ripe pear, Bartlett or Comice**

**2 teaspoons clear honey**

**1/4 cup thick plain yogurt**

**fresh mint sprigs to garnish (optional)**

For the filling (for six):

**2/3 cup whole almonds**

**3 ounces ginger cookies**

**1/4 cup unsalted butter, at room temperature**

**2 tablespoons superfine sugar**

**1 egg yolk**

**juice of 1/2 lemon**

Preheat the oven to 375°F.

Make the filling first. Toast the almonds until golden, either under the broiler, watching them carefully, or in the preheated oven. This only takes a few minutes and really brings out the flavor of the almonds. Chop fairly finely.

Crush the ginger cookies roughly using a rolling pin or the bottom of a small pan. Mix in the almonds, butter, sugar and egg yolk until the ingredients hold together like a rough paste.

Place the lemon juice in a shallow dish. Peel the pear, then roll it in the lemon juice to avoid discoloration. Halve the pear lengthwise and core. Pack a full rounded teaspoonful of the filling onto the hollow of each pear half. This should fill the cavity and cover most of the exposed half. Place the halves in a baking dish and bake in the preheated oven for 15 to 20 minutes, depending on the ripeness and type of pear used. The pear is cooked when the tip of a knife pierces the center easily.

To serve, stir the honey into the yogurt. Place a pear half on each plate and scoop a dollop of the sweetened yogurt beside it. Garnish with mint if desired.

# Tomato Salad
## with Shallots, Balsamic Vinegar and Thyme

A GOOD TOMATO SALAD IS SOMETHING TO REMEMBER. THE SECRET IS GETTING ALL THE SIMPLE THINGS RIGHT. THAT MEANS SUPERB RIPE TOMATOES, SOME FRUITY OLIVE OIL, AND THE RIGHT AMOUNT OF SEASONINGS. LET'S GO! **Serves 2** 

**2 large, ripe, tasty tomatoes**

**salt**

**1/4 teaspoon black peppercorns, cracked**

**1/2 teaspoon fresh thyme leaves**

**crusty bread to serve**

For the dressing:

**2 tablespoons balsamic vinegar**

**5 tablespoons extra-virgin olive oil**

**2 shallots, cut into thin rounds**

**pinch of salt**

To make the dressing, combine all the ingredients in a small bowl and allow it to stand for a least 1 hour. This marinating time pickles the shallots, making them mild and less pungent.

Blanch the tomatoes in boiling water for 12 seconds, then refresh them under cold water. This process loosens the skin and they should now peel very easily. Carefully slice each tomato, keeping the slices together. As each tomato is sliced, transfer it to a plate as you slice it and press it down domino style, one slice overlapping the next. Sprinkle each tomato with a little salt, black pepper and thyme leaves. Now generously spoon over the dressing and serve with some nice crusty bread

# Skate
## with Chili and Basil Cream

Skate is one of the finest-flavored fish in the sea. It's not especially popular in Ireland but that may be due to its appearance, which isn't exactly pretty. Cooked as it is here and served with new potatoes, you'll find it makes one of the most delicious dishes you've ever tasted.

**Serves 2**

**2 skate wings, about 8 ounces each, skinned**

**1 tablespoon unsalted butter**

**2 shallots, finely chopped**

**1/3 cup sliced mushrooms**

**salt**

**1/2 cup dry white wine**

**1/2 cup whipping cream**

**1 fresh red chili, seeded and sliced**

**1 tablespoon chopped fresh basil**

Preheat the oven to 325°F.

Trim 1/2 inch off the tips of the skate wings with a pair of scissors. Butter a large baking sheet and scatter on the shallots and mushrooms. Lay on the skate wings and season with salt. Pour on the wine and cover lightly with foil. Place in the preheated oven and cook for about 20 minutes. The time required will depend on how thick the skate wings are. They are cooked when the flesh comes away easily from the bone. Remove the skate from the oven when cooked. Strain the cooking liquid into a clean pan and keep the fish covered while you make the sauce.

Add the cream and chili to the cooking liquid and bring to a boil. Simmer until the cream thickens to sauce consistency. Add the chopped basil.

To serve, arrange the skate wings on warmed plates with plenty of sauce.

# Spiced Roast Cabbage

THERE ARE MANY WAYS TO SPICE UP THE LOCAL IRISH GRUB. THIS ONE WAS DISCOVERED BY ACCIDENT, BUT WE FIND IT WORKS VERY WELL. CABBAGE, AND IN FACT MOST OF ITS RELATIVES, DOES NOT KEEP VERY WELL WHEN COOKED, SO IT IS NOT A GOOD IDEA TO COOK IT TOO FAR IN ADVANCE. **Serves 2** (V)

**1/4 head savoy cabbage, roughly chopped**

**2 tablespoons unsalted butter**

**1 teaspoon curry powder**

**salt**

Cook the cabbage in boiling salted water for 3 minutes. Drain into a colander, then refresh in cold water. Squeeze the cabbage to remove excess water.

Heat the butter in a large frying pan over medium heat until it foams. Add the cabbage, curry powder and a little salt. Fry for 3 to 4 minutes and serve.

# Peach Crumble
## with Raspberry Cream

SUCH A SCRUMPTIOUS AROMA FILLS THE WHOLE HOUSE WHEN THIS DESSERT IS BAKING IN THE OVEN! IT'S GUARANTEED TO WOO ALL AGES. ALMOST ANY TYPE OF FRUIT CAN BE USED: PEACHES OR NECTARINES, PLUMS OR APPLES, OR TRY TOSSING IN SOME BLACKBERRIES. **Serves 4** (V)

**2 1/2 pounds ripe peaches**

**4 to 6 tablespoons sugar, depending on sweetness of peaches**

**1 tablespoon all-purpose flour**

**grated zest of 1/2 lemon**

**2/3 cup ground almonds**

**2/3 cup sliced almonds**

For the crumble topping:

**1/4 cup superfine sugar**

**1/4 cup light brown sugar**

**3/4 cup all-purpose flour**

**1/2 cup unsalted butter, chilled and diced**

For the raspberry cream:

**1 pint (2 cups) raspberries, fresh or frozen and thawed**

**1/4 cup superfine sugar, or as needed**

**1 teaspoon lemon juice**

**2/3 cup whipping cream**

Preheat the oven to 375°F.

Halve and peel the peaches. Slice each half into 8 wedges. Toss the peaches with the sugar, flour and lemon zest. Set aside.

To make the topping, work together the sugars, flour and butter with your fingertips until they are sticking together in rough bits about pea-size consistency.

Sprinkle the ground almonds over the bottom of a shallow baking dish. Lay the peaches in next; a depth of about 1 inch is most suitable. Generously sprinkle on the crumble topping about 1/2 inch thick. Scatter the sliced almonds over the top. Place in the preheated oven for about 30 minutes, or until the top is golden and a knife will pierce the peach flesh easily. Remove from the oven.

To make the raspberry cream, purée the raspberries and sugar in a blender or food processor. Pass the purée though a fine sieve to remove the seeds. Add the lemon juice to the purée. Whip the cream to soft peaks and fold in the purée. Adjust sweetness if necessary by adding a tablespoon or two more of sugar.

To serve, scoop a big spoonful of the peach crumble into a soup plate or shallow bowl and top with a generous spoonful of the raspberry cream. Serve at once, warm rather than hot.

CHAPTER TWELVE

# Cupid's Cuisine

Many foods throughout the years have been considered a catalyst to love. However, food doesn't have to be an aphrodisiac to reflect your feelings. The time taken to preparc something special shows just how much you care. Remember to keep things rather light, for a big heavy meal is almost guaranteed to send your lover to sleep!

Menu 1

Buttery Stew of Oysters, Asparagus and Leeks

Breast of Chicken Stuffed with Lobster and Basil

Chocolate and Coconut Torte

Menu 2

Cheese Fondue with Asparagus and Broccoli

Salmon Baked with Fresh Herbs and Pommes d'Amour

White Chocolate Mousse with Mandarin Purée

Chocolate Meringues

# Buttery Stew of Oysters, Asparagus and Leeks

THIS IS WHAT WE WOULD CALL A SPONTANEOUS DISH FOR THOSE IN THE MOOD, BECAUSE YOU DO NEED TO BE IN THE MOOD FOR OYSTERS! **Serves 2**

**10 oysters, shucked and reserved in their liquor**

**8 asparagus spears, trimmed and lightly peeled**

**2 tablespoons unsalted butter**

**2 small leeks, thinly sliced**

**1/4 cup water**

**salt and freshly ground white pepper**

**1/4 cup Champagne or dry white wine**

**1/2 cup whipping cream**

**1 teaspoon lemon juice**

**1 teaspoon snipped fresh chives**

**1 teaspoon chopped fresh chervil**

**1 teaspoon chopped fresh parsley**

Check the oysters for pieces of shell. Slice the asparagus on the diagonal into 3/4-inch lengths.

Place a medium pan over high heat. Add the butter, leeks, asparagus and water to the pan with a little salt. Cook at a rapid boil for 4 minutes. Add the Champagne or wine and cook for a further 2 minutes. Add the cream and bring to a boil. Season with salt and pepper. Add the remaining ingredients, including the oysters and their liquor. Allow the oysters to warm for about 30 seconds, then serve in warmed bowls.

# Breast of Chicken
## Stuffed with Lobster and Basil

LOBSTER SEEMS ROMANTIC BECAUSE IT'S SO EXPENSIVE AND EXOTIC. IT IS VERY SEDUCTIVE TO BE WOOED BY THE BEST AND THE MOST EXPENSIVE, SO WE'VE ADDED A BIT OF CHICKEN TO MAKE SURE THAT NO ONE GETS CARRIED AWAY. WE LIKE TO SERVE THIS WITH BUTTERED PASTA. USE FRESH, LIVE LOBSTER IF YOU CAN; IF YOU USE COOKED LOBSTER, MAKE SURE YOU BUY IT VERY FRESH FROM A RELIABLE SOURCE AND OMIT THE FIRST COOKING STAGE. **Serves 2**

**1 lobster, about 1 pound**

**2 large skinless chicken breasts, about 7 ounces each**

**7 tablespoons light cream, chilled**

**1 tablespoon chopped fresh basil**

**1 tablespoon snipped fresh chives**

**salt and freshly ground black pepper**

**1 tablespoon oil**

For the sauce:

**shell from the lobster**

**1 tablespoon olive oil**

**2 shallots, thinly sliced**

**2 garlic cloves, crushed**

**1 tablespoon tomato paste**

**2 tablespoons port**

**2 tablespoons brandy**

**1/4 cup water**

**1 1/4 cups whipping cream**

**1 tablespoon chopped fresh basil**

Preheat the oven to 400°F.

To cook the lobster, bring a large pan of water to a vigorous boil. Put in the lobster, cover and let it cook for about 12 minutes. Remove the lobster from the pan and stop the cooking process by plunging the lobster into a sink of cold water.

Insert a large knife into the lobster at the point where the tail and body are joined and cut toward the tail. The tail meat will now easily pull away from the shell. Break off the arms and claws and crack the shells with a heavy knife. Remove the meat, being careful to discard any pieces of shell. Cut the lobster meat into 1/2-inch dice.

Remove the inside fillets from the chicken breasts. Remove any sinew from these small fillets with a sharp knife and roughly mash the flesh with a heavy knife or in a blender or food processor. Place this mashed chicken in a bowl and add the lobster, cream, basil, chives, salt and pepper. Beat this mixture vigorously with a wooden spoon until it comes together and looks a little sticky.

To prepare the chicken fillets for stuffing, lay each one flat on a cutting board and make a long horizontal incision almost through the breast so that you can open it out like a book. Season each fillet with a little salt and pepper and spoon the lobster stuffing along the middle line. Fold the two sides on top of the stuffing, remolding it into a good shape with your hands. Butter two sheets of aluminum foil each about 10 inches square and wrap each breast tightly, twisting the ends to help keep their shape.

Heat a frying pan over high heat, add the oil, and fry the foil-wrapped fillets for about 4 minutes, turning them every now and then. Place them in the preheated oven for about 15 minutes, then remove them and allow to rest in a warm place.

While the chicken is in the oven, make the sauce. First crush the lobster shells with a heavy cleaver or the household hammer. Fry the shells in a pan with the olive oil over high heat for 2 minutes. Add the shallots and garlic and fry for a further 2 minutes. Add the tomato paste, port, brandy and water and allow this to cook until reduced by half. Add the cream and boil until the sauce thickens. Strain the sauce through a fine sieve into a clean pan and add the chopped basil.

To serve, carefully unwrap the chicken breasts, allowing any juices to fall into the sauce. Slice each breast and arrange attractively on warmed plates. Spoon the sauce generously around.

## Chocolate and Coconut Torte

THERE IS SOMETHING DEFINITELY ROMANTIC ABOUT CHOCOLATE, AND THIS TASTY LITTLE TORTE WILL HAVE YOUR PARTNER SWOONING IN HIS OR HER SEAT. THIS IS A DESSERT DESIGNED TO IMPRESS. IF YOU ARE NOT A COCONUT LOVER, SIMPLY SERVE WITH A TRADITIONAL VANILLA CUSTARD. FOR A MORE ELABORATE PRESENTATION, DRIZZLE A CHOCOLATE SAUCE OVER THE TORTE. **Serves 2** (V)

For the torte:

**4 1/2 ounces bittersweet or semisweet chocolate, finely chopped**

**7 tablespoons unsalted butter**

**3 eggs, separated**

**1/2 cup superfine sugar**

**3 tablespoons all-purpose flour**

**3 or 4 coconut drop macaroons, roughly crushed**

Preheat the oven to 375°F. Grease four 3 1/2-inch molds about 3 inches deep. Line the bottoms with parchment paper.

To start the custard, place the milk and coconut in a pan and bring to a boil. Take off the heat and leave to infuse for at least 30 minutes.

Melt the chocolate in a bowl placed over a small pan of simmering water. Stir in the butter and set aside. Cream the egg yolks with 6 tablespoons of sugar until light and fluffy, then set aside. Whisk the egg whites until they form soft peaks, then add the remaining sugar and whisk vigorously for a further minute or so until the whites are glossy.

Fold the flour gently into the egg yolk mixture, then fold in the melted chocolate, followed by the glossy egg whites. Lastly fold in the crushed macaroons. Fill each mold two-thirds full and bake in the center of the preheated oven for about 15 to 20 minutes. The little tortes are done when a skewer inserted into the center comes out moist but not runny. Remove from the oven and leave to cool in the molds.

To finish the custard, whisk the egg yolks and sugar together in a bowl until light in color and the sugar has dissolved. Strain the coconut milk through a fine sieve. Whisking continuously, slowly pour the strained milk into the egg-sugar mixture.

Pour this mixture back into the pan over low heat and cook for a few minutes, stirring continuously with a wooden spoon until the mixture has thickened enough to coat the back of the spoon and will hold if you run your finger along the middle of the back of the spoon. Strain through a fine sieve, then leave to cool.

To serve, unmold the tortes and place them in the center of individual plates. Surround with the coconut custard and garnish with the toasted coconut flakes and chocolate curls.

For the coconut custard:

**1 cup milk**

**1/4 cup shredded dried coconut**

**3 egg yolks**

**1/3 cup superfine sugar**

**1/4 vanilla bean, split lengthwise, or 1/4 teaspoon vanilla extract**

**1 tablespoon coconut liqueur**

To garnish:

**1/4 cup flaked dried coconut, toasted**

**chocolate curls**

OVERLEAF:

Cupid's Cuisine, Menu 2

Cheese Fondue with Asparagus and Broccoli (page 136)

Salmon Baked with Fresh Herbs and Pommes d'Amour (page 137)

White Chocolate Mousse with Mandarin Purée (page 138)

Chocolate Meringues (page 139)

# Cheese Fondue

## with Asparagus and Broccoli

OUR FRIEND BILL HOGAN IN CORK MUST BE ONE OF IRELAND'S GREATEST CHEESE MAKERS. HE IS PASSIONATE ABOUT SWISS CHEESE MAKING AND, OF COURSE, THE SWISS-STYLE CHEESE FONDUE. HE SHARED WITH US HIS SIMPLE RECIPE USING HIS VERY OWN GRUYÈRE-STYLE CHEESE NAMED AFTER THE LOCAL MOUNTAIN GABRIEL WITH THE SOFT, RATHER SMELLY IRISH DURRUS CHEESE. **Serves 2** (V)

**7 ounces Gruyère-style cheese such as Gabriel, Comte or Emmentaler**

**4 ounces Irish Durrus or Swiss raclette cheese**

**1/2 garlic clove**

**2/3 cup dry white wine**

**freshly ground black pepper**

**7 ounces asparagus spears, cooked**

**7 ounces (about 3 1/2 cups) broccoli florets, cooked**

Cut the cheese into 1/2-inch dice. Rub the inside of a fondue dish with the cut side of the garlic. Add the wine and place the dish over gentle heat. When the wine is warm, add the cheese and stir continuously for about 10 minutes, or until the cheese has melted. Season with pepper. Help yourself to asparagus or broccoli, dipping it into the melted cheese with your fingers.

If the fondue becomes too thick, thin it by adding a few more spoonfuls of wine.

# Salmon Baked
## with Fresh Herbs and Pommes d'Amour

THIS IS A LIGHT AND ATTRACTIVE DISH THAT ALLOWS US TO FINISH WITH A SINFULLY RICH DESSERT. IF YOU WANT TO PREPARE THE DISH IN ADVANCE, WILT THE TOMATOES—THE POMMES D'AMOUR—IN THE OVEN, THEN ALLOW THEM TO COOL IN THE BAKING DISH. ADD THE SALMON, COVER WITH FOIL AND CHILL UNTIL REQUIRED. YOU WILL NEED TO ALLOW AN ADDITIONAL 5 MINUTES OVEN TIME TO MAKE SURE THAT THE DISH WARMS THROUGH. **Serves 2**

**4 ripe tomatoes, peeled**

**1/2 garlic clove, chopped**

**6 tablespoons unsalted butter**

**salt and freshly ground white pepper**

**2 fresh salmon fillets, skinned, about 6 ounces each**

**1 tablespoon lemon juice**

**1 teaspoon fresh tarragon leaves**

**1 teaspoon snipped fresh chives**

**1 teaspoon chopped fresh parsley**

**rice or steamed potatoes to serve**

Preheat the oven to 375°F.

Cut the tomatoes in half and gently squeeze out any seeds. Place them in an 8-by-10-inch baking dish with the garlic, butter and a little salt and pepper. Bake in the preheated oven for 10 minutes, or until the tomatoes are well heated. Season the salmon fillets and add them to the dish, pushing the tomatoes to the outside. Cover with foil and bake for 8 to 10 minutes, or until the salmon is cooked and quite firm. Remove from the oven and mix the lemon juice and the herbs into the buttery tomato juices. Serve on warmed plates with rice or steamed potatoes.

# White Chocolate Mousse
## with Mandarin Purée

IT IS EXTREMELY DIFFICULT TO MAKE THIS MOUSSE IN A SMALLER QUANTITY AND TO STILL GET THE TEXTURE JUST RIGHT. THEREFORE, WE HAVE GIVEN THE RECIPE IN LARGER QUANTITIES SINCE IT FREEZES WELL. THE CHOCOLATE MERINGUES (SEE PAGE 139) MAKE A WONDERFUL BASE FOR THE MOUSSE, OFFERING CONTRASTS OF COLOR AND TEXTURE FOR A MORE COMPLEX AND DRAMATIC DESSERT. **Serves 6 to 8** (V)

For the mousse:

**12 ounces white chocolate, chopped**

**1 1/2 teaspoons powdered gelatin**

**1 tablespoon water**

**2 1/8 cups whipping cream**

**2 eggs**

**1 1/2 tablespoons Napoleon mandarine liqueur**

For the mandarin purée:

**1 can (7 ounces) mandarin segments in light syrup**

**1 1/2 tablespoons Napoleon mandarine liqueur**

**1 tablespoon lemon juice, or to taste**

To decorate:

**fresh mint sprigs**

**mandarin segments (optional)**

To make the mousse, put the white chocolate in a heatproof bowl and place over a saucepan of simmering but not boiling water. Allow to melt, stirring occasionally.

In a small bowl, soften the gelatin in the water for 5 minutes. Whisk the cream until it forms soft peaks; be careful not to whip it too stiffly or the mousse will go dry and granular. Set aside.

Place the eggs in a heatproof mixing bowl and whisk over a pan of simmering water for about 5 minutes until light and fluffy. Add the gelatin mixture to the eggs. Continue to whisk over the bain-marie for another minute to ensure that the gelatin has fully dissolved. Remove from the heat and whisk vigorously for 2 minutes, or until doubled in volume. Whisking gently, add the melted chocolate in a steady stream until well blended. Gently whisk in the softly whipped cream, being sure to reach right to the bottom of the bowl, as the chocolate has a tendency to sink. Finally, fold in the liqueur.

Refrigerate the mousse for at least 2 hours to set. It will keep up to 3 to 4 days in an airtight container in the refrigerator.

To prepare the purée, place all the mandarin pieces and half the syrup from the can in a blender or food processor. Purée, then pass through a fine sieve. Adjust the thickness of the sauce by adding more syrup if necessary. Stir in the liqueur. Add the lemon juice to taste. Set aside.

To serve, use an ice cream scoop or spoon to put 2 dollops of mousse onto each plate. Drizzle the purée around. Decorate with mint and with a mandarin segment, if desired.

# Chocolate Meringues

THESE FEATHERLIGHT DISKS OF MERINGUE HAVE AN INTENSE CHOCOLATE FLAVOR. THEY CAN BE ENJOYED AS A COOKIE OR PETIT FOUR IN THEIR OWN RIGHT, OR SANDWICHED TOGETHER WITH BUTTERCREAM OR GANACHE (A CREAMY CHOCOLATE MIXTURE), OR EVEN USED TO BUILD MORE COMPLEX DESSERTS. THE SIZE AND SHAPE OF THEM CAN BE PIPED ACCORDINGLY. THE MERINGUES CAN BE STORED IN AN AIRTIGHT CONTAINER FOR 7 TO 10 DAYS, SO IT IS WORTH MAKING THIS QUANTITY. **Makes about twelve 3-inch circles** (V)

**3 egg whites**

**1/2 cup plus 1 tablespoon superfine sugar**

**1/2 cup confectioners' sugar, sifted**

**1/3 cup cocoa powder**

Preheat the oven to 225°F. Line a baking sheet with parchment paper.

Gently whisk the egg whites for 30 seconds until they begin to froth. Whisk more vigorously until they start to form soft peaks. In a slow, steady stream, add 6 tablespoons of the superfine sugar. Continue whipping for a further minute until the whites are shiny and thick.

Sift together the rest of the superfine sugar, the confectioners' sugar and cocoa. Fold this mixture into the meringue, ensuring that it's all well mixed together.

Using a pastry bag with a 1/2-inch nozzle, starred or plain, pipe 3-inch rounds onto the parchment paper. Place in the preheated oven and bake slowly for about 2 hours.

These disks should come off the parchment easily and be uniformly crisp when they are sufficiently cooked. Remove from the oven and let cool.

CHAPTER THIRTEEN

# Cup Final Day

At the risk of upsetting some of our women football (soccer) fans, a Cup Final day does tend to be, on the whole, a boys' day out. Therefore we think of recipes of substance, items that go well with beer—in large quantities! It's great to choose dishes that can be made in advance and easily reheated, or even served at room temperature. So give these recipes a go and let the celebrations begin. You'll enjoy yourselves even if you don't end up on the winning side.

### Menu 1

Ham and Cheese Toasties

Cheese Quesadillas

Spicy Avocado Guacamole

Pork Ribs with Spiced Apple Glaze

Persian Rice Pilau

Chocolate and Banana Ice Cream Pie with Fudge Sauce

### Menu 2

Blackened Chicken

Baked Macaroni with Zucchini, Mushrooms and Cheese

Death by Chocolate

# Ham and Cheese Toasties

ONE OF THOSE ALL-ROUND FAVORITES, THIS RECIPE CAN BE VARIED TO SUIT YOUR TASTE; IF YOU PREFER CHEESE AND TOMATO, GO FOR IT! OR TRY AVOCADO AND ALFALFA SPROUTS AND CHEESE, AND SO ON AND SO ON! **Makes 8**

**16 slices bread**

**1/2 cup unsalted butter, at room temperature**

**12 ounces Gouda cheese, thinly sliced**

**12 ounces ham, sliced**

**freshly ground black pepper**

Preheat a cast iron frying pan over medium heat.

Generously butter one side of each of the slices of bread. Place 1 slice of bread, butter-side down, into the warm pan. Quickly arrange the cheese and ham slices onto the slice. Season well with the freshly ground pepper and top with another slice butter-side up. Cook over a medium heat for about 2 to 3 minutes, or until the bottom bread slice is nice and golden. Carefully flip the toasties over and cook on the second side for a further 2 minutes. Lift this toastie out, keep it warm in a low oven and continue to make the rest of the toasties.

To serve, remove the toasties from the oven and cut each one in half. Serve at once.

OVERLEAF:
Cup Final Day, Menu 1
Ham and Cheese Toasties (page 141)
Cheese Quesadillas (page 144)
Spicy Avocado Guacamole (page 145)
Pork Ribs with Spiced Apple Glaze (page 146)
Persian Rice Pilau (page 147)
Chocolate and Banana Ice Cream Pie with Fudge Sauce (page 148)

# Cheese Quesadillas

CHEESE QUESADILLAS ARE ONE OF THOSE SNACK FOODS THAT ARE EXTREMELY ADDICTIVE. THEY'RE QUICK TO MAKE, NUTRITIOUS AND TASTY. KIDS AND ADULTS LOVE THEM, AND YOU CAN PUT WHATEVER YOU FANCY INTO THEM. YOU CAN BUY READY-MADE TORTILLAS IN GOOD SUPERMARKETS AND DELICATESSENS, AND PICK UP SOME TOMATO SALSA, TOO, TO SERVE WITH WITH CHEESE QUESADILLAS AND THE SPICY AVOCADO GUACAMOLE (SEE PAGE 145). **Serves 8** (V)

**16 flour tortillas**

**4 tablespoons vegetable oil**

**4 tablespoons unsalted butter**

**1 3/4 pounds Gouda or Cheddar cheese, grated**

Preheat the oven to 300°F.

Preheat a heavy-based frying-pan over medium heat. The butter should sizzle on contact when added. Add 12 tablespoon of butter and 12 tablespoon of oil to the pan. As it melts, lay a tortilla in the pan and quickly sprinkle a handful of the grated cheese into the center of the tortilla. If it's falling over the edges it will just stick to the pan as it cooks. Lay another tortilla on top and cook over medium heat for about 2 minutes. The bottom tortilla should be golden brown. Flip over and cook for another minute or so. By the time the second tortilla is golden brown, the cheese should be well melted.

Transfer the tortilla from the frying pan to some paper towels to remove any excess grease. Place in an ovenproof dish in the preheated oven and proceed to cook the other quesadillas in the same way.

# Spicy Avocado Guacamole

This dip has many options. Leave out the chili or the tomatoes; add finely minced onion or green bell pepper. Whichever way you prefer it, you'll find it handy as a dip for vegetable crudités or quesadillas and as a spread for sandwiches. It tastes best with plum tomatoes. **Serves 8 as a dip or condiment** (V)

**3 ripe avocados, peeled**

**juice of 2 limes**

**1 garlic clove, finely chopped**

**5 plum tomatoes, peeled, seeded and chopped**

**2 tablespoons chopped fresh cilantro**

**1 or 2 fresh red or green chilies, seeded and finely chopped**

**salt and freshly ground white pepper**

In a small stainless steel or glass bowl, mash the avocado flesh until it is a rough, slightly lumpy purée. A potato masher does a great job, but a wooden spoon will suffice as well. Stir in the lime juice immediately, as this preserves the color. Stir in the garlic, tomatoes and cilantro.

Then add the chilies, but remember when adding fresh chili it is very hard to give exact amounts because the variety of chili will make a big difference. A general rule of thumb is that green tend to be hotter than red, and smaller are hotter than larger chilies. The best way to approach it is add half a chili first, taste and adjust as you prefer. Give the avocado a few minutes to absorb the chili flavour after each addition. Add the salt and pepper to taste.

Use immediately or cover with plastic wrap and place in the refrigerator for up to 2 to 3 days.

# Pork Ribs
## with Spiced Apple Glaze

THIS IS ONE OF THOSE RECIPES WHERE YOU THROW EVERYTHING IN A ROASTING PAN, PUT IT IN THE OVEN, SHAKE IT EVERY NOW AND THEN, AND 1 1/2 HOURS LATER YOU HAVE SOMETHING WONDERFUL. IT WILL EMERGE BEAUTIFULLY TENDER WITH A SHINY GLAZE AND EXOTIC FRUIT AROMAS. **Serves 8**

**5 pounds pork ribs**

**2 tablespoons salt**

**2 garlic cloves, finely chopped**

**3 tablespoons peeled and grated fresh ginger**

**3 tablespoons soy sauce**

**2 1/2 cups apple juice**

**1 large cooking apple, peeled, cored and sliced**

**1 tablespoon red pepper flakes**

**4 tablespoons Demerara sugar or other coarse raw sugar**

About 2 hours before cooking (or the night before), season the ribs with the salt, place them in 2 large roasting pans and leave to stand.

Preheat the oven to 400°F.

Mix the remaining ingredients in a large bowl and pour over the ribs. Cover each pan with foil and place in the preheated oven for 1 hour. Remove the foil, give each pan a shake and baste the ribs with the juices. Return to the oven without the foil and allow the liquids to reduce to a shining glaze. Continue basting the ribs every 5 to 10 minutes or so until all the liquid is reduced. Remove from the oven and allow to cool slightly. Chop each side into several portions and serve with finger bowls and plenty of napkins.

# Persian Rice Pilau

THE FLAVORS OF THIS RICE PILAU ADD REAL PIZZAZZ—ESPECIALLY TO THOSE WHO FIND PLAIN RICE BLAND. IT CAN ALSO BE COOKED GENTLY ON TOP OF THE STOVE RATHER THAN IN THE OVEN, IF YOU PREFER. THE AMOUNT OF SALT WILL REALLY DEPEND ON THE VEGETABLE STOCK USED. SOME ARE SO SALTY THAT YOU WILL NOT HAVE TO ADD ANY MORE. TASTE THE RICE WHEN YOU REMOVE IT FROM THE OVEN, AND ADD A LITTLE MORE SALT IF NECESSARY WITH THE RAISINS AND LEMON ZEST. **Serves 8** (V)

**7 ounces onions, finely chopped**

**1 cup (8 ounces) unsalted butter**

**1 cinnamon stick**

**1 bay leaf**

**1 tablespoon peeled and finely chopped fresh ginger**

**1 tablespoon curry powder**

**3 cups long-grain white rice**

**7 cups vegetable stock, boiling**

**2/3 cup golden raisins**

**grated zest of 1 lemon**

**salt**

**1 cup pine nuts, lightly toasted**

Preheat the oven to 350°F.

In a large, heavy-based ovenproof pan, cook the onions in the butter over medium heat for about 5 minutes, or until they are soft and transparent. Add the cinnamon, bay leaf, ginger and curry powder and cook gently for another minute.

Add the rice and hot vegetable stock. Bring to a boil over medium to high heat. Cover with a tight-fitting lid and place in the preheated oven for about 10 to 15 minutes, or until the rice is tender. Remove from the oven and stir in the raisins and lemon zest and salt if necessary. Replace the cover and leave the rice to steam in its own heat for 5 minutes. Just before serving, garnish with the toasted pine nuts.

# Chocolate and Banana Ice Cream Pie
## with Fudge Sauce

ALTHOUGH THIS ICE CREAM PIE TAKES A BIT OF TIME AND ORGANIZATION TO MAKE, IT'S A GREAT DESSERT FOR A LARGE GATHERING. IT CAN BE MADE A DAY OR TWO AHEAD AND THEN SERVED UP WITH NO FUSS ON THE DAY. THIS WICKED FUDGE SAUCE IS GREAT TO HAVE IN THE REFRIGERATOR TO SERVE WITH SIMPLE BOWLS OF ICE CREAM, TOO! IN THE STATES, THIS STYLE OF ICE CREAM PIE IS FREQUENTLY KNOW AS A MUD PIE. MORE THAN 6 HOURS IN THE FREEZER WILL SET THE ICE CREAM PIE SOLID, SO IT MUST BE ALLOWED TO "SOFTEN" BEFORE SERVING. THE SAFEST WAY TO DO THIS IS TO PLACE IT IN THE REFRIGERATOR FOR 2 TO 3 HOURS BEFORE SERVING. THE PIE KEEPS WELL IN THE FREEZER IF WRAPPED TIGHTLY IN PLASTIC WRAP, SO MAKE THE FULL AMOUNT AND YOU'LL HAVE SOME FOR ANOTHER OCCASION. **Serves 10 to 12** (V)

For the base:

**1 1/4 cups pecans**

**5 ounces plain graham crackers**

**1/2 cup unsalted butter, melted**

**2 tablespoons superfine sugar**

For the filling:

**1 cup water**

**1 1/4 cups superfine sugar**

**8 egg yolks**

**7 ounces milk chocolate or semisweet chocolate**

**4 bananas, very ripe**

**1 tablespoon unsalted butter**

**2 tablespoons rum or whiskey (optional)**

**4 cups whipping cream**

Preheat the oven to 375°F. Grease a 10-inch springform pan and line the bottom with parchment paper.

If you wish to enhance the flavor of the pecans, toast them in the preheated oven for 10 to 15 minutes.

To make the base, place all the ingredients in a blender or food processor and process until well mixed. Pat this base into the bottom of the prepared pan so that it is about 1/4 inch thick on the bottom. Pat it about 3/4 inch up the sides of the pan. Set aside.

To make the filling, place the water and sugar in a small pan and bring to a boil; the sugar will dissolve. Let this syrup cool slightly.

Place the egg yolks in a large bowl that will sit well above a big pan a one-quarter full of simmering but not boiling water. Don't put the bowl over the water yet, just have it all ready. Melt the chocolate either in a microwave or over a small pan of hot but not boiling water. Set aside.

Peel and roughly chop the bananas. Heat a small frying pan over medium heat, add the butter and bananas. Cook until the bananas are very soft and mushy. Take off the heat, add the rum or whiskey, if using, and with a potato masher or a fork, mash the cooked banana to a smooth purée. Set aside.

Whip the cream to soft peaks.

For the fudge sauce:

**4 1/2 ounces semisweet chocolate, finely chopped**

**3 tablespoons superfine sugar**

**1/4 cup corn syrup**

**1/4 cup water**

**1/3 cup cocoa powder**

**2 tablespoons rum or whiskey (optional)**

Whisking continuously, slowly pour the hot syrup onto the egg yolks and place the mixture over the prepared pan of simmering water. Continue to whisk for about 10 minutes, or until the mixture is pale yellow, has quadrupled in volume and trails off the whisk in ribbons. Starting with the syrup fairly hot will take much less time than if the syrup has cooled to room temperature.

Remove from the heat and continue gently whisking this fluffy mixture for several minutes over a large bowl of iced water until cool. Fold in the whipped cream and split the whole mixture equally between 2 bowls. Fold the melted chocolate into one bowl and the banana purée into the other.

Pour the chocolate filling into the springform pan first; it should fill it about half full. Gently pour the banana mixture over the top until the pan is full. Place in the freezer for about 3 hours, or until set.

To make the fudge sauce, melt the chopped chocolate either in the microwave or in a bowl over a pan of just simmering water. Meanwhile, boil the other ingredients for 1 to 2 minutes, stirring constantly. Remove from the heat and leave to cool slightly. Stir in the melted chocolate and rum or whiskey if using. This sauce keeps well in the refrigerator. Simply heat up in the microwave or heat gently over a small pan of hot water.

To serve, run a hot knife around the edges of the pan and remove the ring. Using a hot knife, cut slices of the ice cream pie and place on individual plates. Serve with the warm fudge sauce.

# Blackened Chicken

CHICKEN CAN BE A LITTLE DULL SOMETIMES, BUT NOT SO WITH THIS EXPLOSIVE RECIPE. THE LOUISIANA-STYLE SPICES GIVE US A VERITABLE TORRENT OF FLAVORS. FABULOUS HOT OR COLD, THIS ONE IS A WINNER! **Serves 8**

**8 large skinless chicken fillets, about 7 ounces each**

**1/4 cup vegetable oil**

**salad leaves or watercress sprigs to garnish**

Blackening spices:

**2 teaspoons salt**

**2 teaspoons dried oregano**

**2 teaspoons dried thyme**

**1 teaspoon black pepper**

**1 teaspoon white pepper**

**1 teaspoon onion powder**

**1 teaspoon garlic powder**

**1 teaspoon paprika**

**1 teaspoon cayenne pepper**

Preheat the oven to 400°F.

In a large bowl, mix together all the blackening spices. Toss the chicken in the spices, making sure that each fillet is evenly coated. Heat a large, heavy frying pan over high heat until very hot. Add the oil and fry the chicken fillets on each side. You want the chicken to fry quite fast so that you sear and roast the spices very well. Don't be tempted to add too many fillets to the pan at once or you will not get the desired effect. When each fillet is well seared, place in a roasting pan and bake in the preheated oven for 10 minutes.

Serve the chicken on a platter garnished with a few salad leaves or watercress.

# Baked Macaroni
## with Zucchini, Mushrooms and Cheese

MACARONI SHOULD NEVER GO OUT OF FASHION. COOKING A DISH LIKE THIS REMINDS YOU HOW SATISFYING AND VERSATILE THIS LITTLE PASTA SHAPE IS. OF COURSE, YOU MAY USE PENNE, RIGATONI, FUSILLI OR WHATEVER OTHER SHAPE YOU CHOOSE, BUT SOMEHOW THEY ARE NOT QUITE AS COMFORTING. **Serves 8** 

Preheat the oven to 375°F. Lightly butter a large baking dish about 14 by 8 inches.

Heat half the oil and 2 tablespoons of butter in a large frying pan over high heat until the butter is foaming. Add the zucchini, season with a little salt and pepper and fry until lightly browned and just cooked. Tip the zucchini into a colander, then fry the mushrooms in the same way, using the remaining 2 tablespoons oil and 2 tablespoons of butter.

Bring about 5 quarts of salted water to a boil in a large pan. Add the macaroni, stir well and cook until just al dente. Drain well.

While the macaroni is draining, add the remaining 1/2 cup plus 2 tablespoons butter and cream to the pan and bring to a boil. Return the macaroni to the pan with the mushrooms, zucchini and half the cheeses. Check and adjust the seasoning to taste. Tip everything into the baking dish. Sprinkle with the remaining cheese and bake in the preheated oven for about 15 minutes.

**4 tablespoons olive oil**

**3/4 cup plus 2 tablespoons unsalted butter**

**8 medium zucchini, cut into 3/4-inch dice**

**salt and freshly ground black pepper**

**1 1/2 pounds button mushrooms, quartered**

**1 1/4 pounds macaroni**

**2 cups whipping cream**

**2 cups grated mild Cheddar cheese**

**2 cups grated Parmesan cheese**

# Death by Chocolate

THIS IS ONE DESSERT THAT WILL SATISFY EVEN THE MOST DIE-HARD CHOCOHOLIC: SMOOTH, INTENSE AND INDESCRIBABLY DELICIOUS! TRY IT AND SEE. IF YOU WISH, THE TERRINE CAN BE DECORATED WITH WHIPPED CREAM, RASPBERRY SAUCE (SEE PAGE 80) OR EVEN CHOCOLATE SAUCE (SEE PAGE 183). **Serves 8 to 10** 

**1 pound bittersweet or semisweet chocolate, chopped**

**1 cup whipping cream**

**1/4 cup unsalted butter**

**4 egg yolks**

**1 1/4 cups confectioners' sugar, sifted**

**1/2 cup Irish whiskey or liqueur**

Line a 1-quart terrine with plastic wrap, letting it hang generously over all four sides.

Place the chocolate, cream and butter in a medium bowl and place over a pan of just simmering water. Stir occasionally until the chocolate and butter have melted and mixed together. Remove from the heat and slowly whisk in the egg yolks. Slowly stir in the confectioners' sugar and continue to stir gently until the mixture is smooth, shiny and homogenous. Stir in the whiskey or your chosen liqueur.

Pour into the prepared terrine and smooth out to fill the mold. Tap the mold on the worktop once or twice to remove any air bubbles. Cover with the plastic wrap and chill overnight.

To serve, unmold by turning upside down onto a chopping board or other flat surface. Cut into slices with a hot knife.

CHAPTER FOURTEEN

# Lean Times

Our society is in the grip of a fitness and health revival. This can be intimidating at first because there is a lot to think about: How do I cook low-fat food? How can I become nutritionally aware? Take it one step at a time. It's surprising how easy it can be when you understand the basic breakdown of foodstuffs. You'll notice right away that herbs, spices and flavorings become a very important and exciting part of dishes.

### Menu 1

Carrageen Tomato Mousse

Salad of Green Beans

Ostrich Satay

Savory Vegetable Pancakes

Ruby Grapefruit and Juniper Granita

### Menu 2

Mussels with Potato and Garlic

Grilled Chicken with Lemon, Black Pepper and Red Onion

Warm Lentil and Fennel Salad

Fresh Papaya with Coconut Yogurt Cream

# Carrageen Tomato Mousse

Carrageen is an Irish seaweed that is well known for its gelatinous and nutritious qualities. If properly prepared it doesn't taste at all of the sea and can even be used in desserts. It is available in some health-food shops. **Serves 4 to 6** (V)

**1 ounce carrageen moss or 4 teaspoons powdered gelatin**

**1 tablespoon light olive oil**

**2 tablespoons shallots, sliced**

**1 tablespoon chopped garlic**

**1 1/4 pounds very ripe tomatoes, quartered**

**1/4 cup tomato paste**

**1/2 large red bell pepper, seeded and sliced**

**1 tablespoon tomato ketchup**

**20 drops Tabasco sauce**

**1 tablespoon chopped fresh tarragon**

**5 egg whites**

**salt and freshly ground black pepper**

Wash the carrageen moss and soak it in cold water for about 30 minutes or until it swells to double its size. Drain it in a colander and squeeze dry. It is now ready to use. Alternatively, dissolve the gelatin in a little cold water.

In a large pan, heat the oil and cook the shallots and garlic for about 3 minutes, or until soft. Add the remaining ingredients except the carrageen moss or gelatin, tarragon and egg whites. Add a little salt and mash the tomatoes with a spoon to encourage them to release their juice. Bring to a boil and simmer for about 5 minutes. Add the carrageen moss or gelatin, cover and cook gently for 15 minutes. Tip the tomato mixture into a blender or food processor and purée until smooth. Pass through a sieve into a clean bowl, add the tarragon and a little pepper and allow to cool to room temperature.

Whisk the egg whites in a clean bowl until they form soft peaks. Fold about one-third of the egg whites into the tomato mixture with a spatula. Then carefully fold in the remainder, cover and chill for at least 6 hours.

To serve, dip a soup spoon or an ice cream scoop into hot water, then scoop the mousse into the center of individual plates.

# Salad of Green Beans

WHEN PROPERLY PREPARED, A SIMPLE SALAD OF GREEN BEANS CAN BE STUNNING. WE FEEL THAT IT IS IMPORTANT TO COOK THE BEANS ENOUGH SO THAT THEY ARE NOT CRUNCHY OR SQUEAKY TO EAT. COOKED UNTIL JUST TENDER, THEY HAVE MUCH MORE FLAVOR AND CHARACTER. IF YOU ARE PREPARING THIS IN ADVANCE, DON'T COMBINE THE BEANS WITH THE DRESSING UNTIL THE LAST MOMENT OR THEY WILL GO GRAY.

**Serves 4** 

**7 ounces green beans**

**2 shallots, finely chopped**

**1/2 teaspoon finely chopped garlic**

**1/4 cup Standard Vinaigrette (see page 178)**

**salt and freshly ground black pepper**

Bring a pan of lightly salted water to the boil. Taste the water. If it doesn't taste lightly salty, add more salt. Add the green beans and cook at a rolling boil for about 8 to 10 minutes, or until tender. Drain in a colander, refresh in plenty of cold water, then allow to cool while you make the dressing.

In a small bowl combine the shallots, garlic and vinaigrette. Add the beans to the dressing and toss to coat evenly. Serve immediately with salt to taste and a few twists of pepper.

# Ostrich Satay

IRISH OSTRICH FARMERS ARE HAILING OSTRICH AS THE PERFECT MEAT. LOWER IN FAT THAN CHICKEN AND HIGHER IN PROTEIN THAN BEEF, IT VERY WELL MIGHT BE. ALL OF OUR "GUINEA PIGS" LOVED IT, PROCLAIMING IT TO BE QUITE LIKE BEEF. NEEDLESS TO SAY YOU CAN SUBSTITUTE BEEF FILLET FOR THE OSTRICH VERY SUCCESSFULLY. SNOW PEAS OR SUGAR SNAP PEAS MAKE A GOOD ACCOMPANIMENT. **Serves 4**

**1 1/2 pounds ostrich or beef fillet**
**1 tablespoon vegetable oil**

For the marinade:
**1/4 cup dark soy sauce**
**1 1/2 tablespoons curry powder**
**2 tablespoons clear honey**
**pinch of white pepper**
**1 tablespoon peanut oil**

Slice the fillet into 8 medallions. Combine all the marinade ingredients in a bowl. Add the meat, rubbing the marinade into the meat with your fingers. Cover and allow the meat to marinate for a least 4 hours or preferably overnight in the refrigerator.

Heat a large nonstick frying pan over high heat. Add a little vegetable oil, then 4 medallions and cook for about 2 minutes on each side for medium rare or 4 minutes for well done. Allow the medallions to rest in a warm place while you finish cooking the remaining pieces. When all are cooked, scrape any remaining marinade into the pan and add a few tablespoons of water. This will give a little bit of sauce to drizzle over the finished dish.

# Savory Vegetable Pancakes

THESE LEAN, HIGH-FIBER PANCAKES ARE THE PERFECT ACCOMPANIMENT TO GRILLED MEATS, OR THEY WOULD ALSO WORK WELL WITH ASIAN FISH RECIPES LIKE THE GLAZED MONKFISH WITH BLACK PEPPER AND GINGER (SEE PAGE 79). **Serves 4 to 6** (V)

**1 egg white**

**salt**

**1/2 garlic clove, crushed and chopped**

**7 ounces zucchini, grated**

**4 ounces carrots, grated**

**4 ounces celeriac, grated**

**4 ounces mushrooms, finely chopped**

**1 tablespoon chopped onion**

**1 teaspoon peeled and finely grated fresh ginger**

**1/4 teaspoon curry powder**

**3 tablespoons dried bread crumbs**

**2 tablespoons whole-wheat flour**

**freshly ground black pepper**

**4 tablespoons vegetable oil**

Lightly whisk the egg white with a pinch of salt and the garlic. Add the remaining ingredients except the vegetable oil.

Heat a large nonstick frying pan over medium heat. Brush a little of the oil over the frying pan. Drop 2-tablespoon mounds of the pancake mixture into the pan. Pat each mound out to form a pancake about 2 1/2 inches in diameter. Cook the pancakes for about 3 minutes on each side, or until they are lightly browned. Transfer the pancakes to a baking sheet and keep them warm in a low oven. Cook the remaining mixture in the same way.

# Ruby Grapefruit and Juniper Granita

The clear, unadulterated flavor of this granita is immensely refreshing. In fact it's one of Paul's favorite desserts. Pure and simple. Use tall wide-rimmed glasses like martini glasses if possible, and chill them before serving so that the granita does not melt so quickly.

**Serves 4 to 6** 

**1 1/2 cups water**

**1 cup superfine sugar**

**about 6 juniper berries, lightly crushed**

**2 ruby grapefruit**

**1 cup fresh ruby grapefruit juice**

**1 1/2 tablespoons gin**

Place 1/2 cup of water, 1/4 cup of sugar and the juniper berries in a pan and bring to a boil. Remove from the heat and leave to infuse for 30 minutes.

In another small pan, bring the remaining water and sugar to a boil, then remove from the heat and leave to cool.

Segment the grapefruit so as to remove all the skin, pith and seeds. Place the grapefruit segments in the second sugar solution and chill in the refrigerator.

Strain the sugar water and juniper berries through a fine sieve into the grapefruit juice, then add the gin. Pour this into a wide shallow metal container and place in the freezer for about 1 hour, or until the granita starts to freeze and form crystals. Scrape the sides and mix gently to combine the more frozen parts with the less frozen. A true granita texture is formed by stirring occasionally while freezing; this forms the tiny crystals of ice. It will take about 3 hours for it all to set sufficiently.

To serve, place a few of the grapefruit segments in each glass. Scoop in a spoonful or two of the granita and top with a couple more segments. Serve at once!

# Mussels
## with Potato and Garlic

MUSSELS ARE SO TASTY THAT THEY REQUIRE VERY LITTLE EMBELLISHMENT. HERE THEY ARE PARTNERED WITH GARLIC POTATOES AND HERBS TO GIVE A GUTSY LOW-FAT TREAT. IT IS IMPORTANT NOT TO BOIL THE MUSSELS TOO MUCH OR THEY WILL BECOME TOUGH. ADD A SPLASH OF CREAM AT THE LAST MOMENT FOR EXTRA LUXURY.

**Serves 4**

**3 1/2 pounds live mussels**

**scant 1 cup water**

**1/4 cup dry white wine**

**1 fresh thyme sprig**

**1 fresh parsley sprig**

**3 garlic cloves, sliced**

**4 ounces leeks, thinly sliced**

**14 ounces potatoes, peeled and cut into 1/2-inch dice**

**1 tablespoon chopped fresh parsley**

**freshly ground black pepper**

Wash the mussels in plenty of cold water, pulling away the hairy beards as you go. Discard any that are not closed or do not close when tapped sharply with a knife. Bring the water and white wine to a boil in a large pan. Add the herb sprigs and garlic and simmer for 1 minute. Add the mussels, bring to a vigorous boil and cook for 4 to 5 minutes, or until they have all opened. Discard any mussels that have not opened. Immediately drain into a colander, catching all the juices in a bowl underneath.

Strain the juices through a fine sieve into a clean pan and add the leeks and potatoes. Cook over medium heat for about 7 minutes, or until the potatoes are tender.

While the potatoes are cooking, pull the mussels from their shells. Save a few of the shells for garnish.

To serve, add the mussels and chopped parsley to the potato broth and warm thoroughly. Check and adjust the seasoning to taste. Serve in warmed bowls garnished with a few nice shells.

# Grilled Chicken

## with Lemon, Black Pepper and Red Onion

THIS ZESTY LITTLE DISH CAN BE WHIPPED UP IN MINUTES, BUT IT DOES IMPROVE IF YOU HAVE THE TIME TO LET IT MARINATE. YOU CAN FIND PRESERVED LEMONS IN MOST LARGE SUPERMARKETS AND IN ASIAN OR MIDDLE EASTERN GROCERIES. **Serves 4**

**4 skinless chicken breast fillets, about 7 ounces each**

**1 preserved lemon, finely chopped**

**1 red onion, finely chopped**

**1 teaspoon black pepper, cracked**

**1/2 teaspoon red pepper flakes (optional)**

**1 tablespoon chopped fresh parsley**

**2 tablespoons olive oil**

**1 teaspoon clear honey**

**1 teaspoon salt**

**a few mixed salad leaves to serve**

Preheat the broiler to its highest setting.

Combine all the ingredients in a large bowl and toss thoroughly. If you have the time, cover and allow it to marinate for a few hours in the refrigerator.

Place the chicken flat on a broiler pan. Make sure that the chicken pieces are well coated with the little pieces of onion and lemon and so on, as this gives a beautiful color. Place under the grill and cook for 7 to 10 minutes on each side, or until the chicken is firm and completely cooked. Serve garnished with a few mixed salad leaves.

# Warm Lentil and Fennel Salad

LENTILS ARE DEFINITELY ONE OF THE FOODS OF THE MOMENT. BROWN OR GREEN LENTILS WORK BEST FOR THIS RECIPE, AND BOTH ARE READILY AVAILABLE. THIS SALAD CAN EASILY BE MADE A DAY OR TWO AHEAD AND THEN SERVED WARM OR COLD. **Serves 4** (V)

**1 1/8 cups dried green lentils**

**2 1/2 cups water**

**1 teaspoon salt**

**1 fresh thyme sprig**

**1/2 teaspoon dried thyme**

**1 fresh parsley sprig**

**1 small onion, finely chopped**

**1 small carrot, finely chopped**

**1 fennel bulb, finely chopped**

**3 tablespoons balsamic vinegar or 1 1/2 tablespoons white wine vinegar**

**5 tablespoons olive oil**

**1 tablespoon chopped fresh parsley**

**1 teaspoon black peppercorns, cracked**

Rinse the lentils in plenty of cold water. Place them in a pan with the water and salt. Bring to a boil and simmer for 5 minutes, skimming off any scum that rises to the surface. Add the herb sprigs and vegetables and simmer for a further 15 minutes, by which time the lentils should be cooked. Drain off any excess water and allow the lentils to cool slightly. Finally, stir in the remaining ingredients and serve warm.

OVERLEAF:

Lean Times, Menu 2

Mussels with Potato and Garlic (page 159)

Grilled Chicken with Lemon, Black Pepper and Red Onion (page 160)

Warm Lentil and Fennel Salad (page 161)

Fresh Papaya with Coconut Yogurt Cream (page 164)

TEFAL

52
53
54
3

# Fresh Papaya
## with Coconut Yogurt Cream

GOOD-QUALITY PAPAYAS ARE WIDELY AVAILABLE NOW; JUST BE SURE TO USE RIPE ONES, AS THEIR FLAVOR WILL BE FULLY DEVELOPED. WHAT COULD BE SIMPLER THAN SLICING UP A GORGEOUS PIECE OF FRUIT AND DRESSING IT WITH COMPLEMENTARY FLAVORS? MANGOES COULD BE SUBSTITUTED FOR A CHANGE. **Serves 4** (V)

**2 ripe papayas**

**juice of 1 lime**

**1/2 to 1 cup coconut milk**

**1 cup thick plain yogurt**

**3 to 4 tablespoons superfine sugar**

**2 tablespoons flaked dried coconut, toasted (optional)**

Halve, seed and peel the papayas. Slice each half attractively and arrange on individual serving plates. Sprinkle liberally with lime juice to taste.

Stir about 1/2 cup of coconut milk into the yogurt. Taste. Each brand of coconut milk seems to be different, so this is a starting amount. Add more as needed. A couple tablespoons of sugar really brings up the flavors (although not absolutely necessary if you're on a strict diet), so stir in 3 to 4 tablespoons of sugar and taste again. Really just a hint of sweetness is all the cream needs.

Scoop a dollop of the yogurt cream onto each plate beside the papaya slices and decorate with toasted coconut flakes if desired.

CHAPTER FIFTEEN

# Meatless Meals

Many carnivores have never eaten a good vegetarian meal, and believe that if they gave up meat they would suffer nutritionally. This is false. A good vegetarian meal can be completely satisfying. There are no dietary problems with a sound vegetarian diet: with proper knowledge it can be as balanced as any. With today's low standard of health and the high cost of meat, perhaps it's an issue that more people should be thinking about.

Menu 1

Roast Pumpkin Soup with Fresh Thyme

Gruyère and Parmesan Cheese Toasts

Risotto Primavera

Salad of Herbs

Buttered Apples on Sugar-Glazed Barmbrack

Menu 2

Mushroom and Eggplant Tart with Garlic Chives

Penne with Broccoli, Goat Cheese and Sun-Dried Tomatoes

Kiwifruit Soup with Passion Fruit Ice Cream

# Roast Pumpkin Soup
## with Fresh Thyme

PUMPKIN IS A WONDERFUL WINTER VEGETABLE THAT LENDS ITSELF TO A GREAT VARIETY OF RECIPES. IT'S WORTH GETTING TO KNOW, AND THIS SOUP IS A GOOD STARTING POINT. EXPERIMENT WITH DIFFERENT VARIETIES, AS SOME CAN BE VERY BLAND WHILE OTHERS ARE RICH AND CONCENTRATED. BUTTERNUT AND ACORN ARE TWO OF OUR FAVORITES. THE SOUP WILL KEEP IN AN AIRTIGHT CONTAINER IN THE REFRIGERATOR FOR SEVERAL DAYS. **Serves 6** (V)

**1 pumpkin, 2 1/4 pounds, halved and seeded**

**4 1/2 tablespoons unsalted butter**

**1 1/2 pounds onions, roughly chopped**

**3 garlic cloves, finely chopped**

**3 cups vegetable stock**

**1 bouquet garni (leek, bay leaf, parsley, thyme, black peppercorns)**

**pinch of freshly grated nutmeg**

**pinch of cayenne pepper**

**salt and freshly ground white pepper**

**1 1/2 cups milk**

**1 tablespoon fresh thyme leaves or 1/2 tablespoon dried thyme**

**Gruyère and Parmesan Cheese Toasts (see page 167) to serve**

Preheat the oven to 400°F.

Place the pieces of seeded pumpkin flesh-side down on a large baking sheet. Cover tightly with foil and cook in the preheated oven for about 1 hour, or until the flesh is soft to the touch. Remove from the oven, scoop all the flesh off the pumpkin shell and set aside.

Melt the butter in a large pan over medium high heat and cook the onions and garlic for about 5 minutes, until soft and translucent without any coloring. Add the cooked pumpkin flesh and vegetable stock and all the seasonings except the thyme. Bring to a boil, then simmer gently for about 10 minutes. As the pumpkin and onion are already cooked, you're really just letting the flavors meld together at this point. Remove from the heat and leave to cool slightly. Purée in a blender or food processor, then pass through a fine sieve.

Return to a clean pan, add the milk and thyme, then reheat the soup over medium heat without allowing it to boil. Serve immediately in warmed soup bowls with the Gruyère and Parmesan Cheese Toasts on the side, or even placed on top just before serving.

# Gruyère and Parmesan Cheese Toasts

A GRILLED CHEESE TOAST IS SO SIMPLE AND YET SO TASTY. SERVE WITH SOUP, OR EVEN FLOATING ON A SOUP, WITH A SALAD OR SIMPLE VEGETABLE DISH. THE PASTE KEEPS WELL IN THE REFRIGERATOR FOR SEVERAL DAYS AND CAN BE EXTREMELY USEFUL TO HAVE ON HAND. **Serves 6** (V)

**4 ounces Gruyère cheese, finely grated**

**3/4 cup grated Parmesan cheese**

**1/2 cup plus 1 tablespoon unsalted butter, softened**

**6 slices country-style bread, each 3/4 inch thick**

Preheat the broiler.

In a bowl, work the 2 cheeses together with the butter until you have a cohesive paste. Lightly toast the bread slices on both sides. Spread a generous amount of the cheese paste onto each slice, at least 1/4 inch thick. Place the toasts under the broiler for 1 to 2 minutes and watch carefully. They are done when the top is golden brown and bubbly. Serve immediately.

# Risotto Primavera

A CREAMY RISOTTO LIKE THIS CAN LEND ITSELF TO ANY MIXTURE OF VEGETABLES, SO FEEL FREE TO EXPERIMENT AND USE WHAT YOU PREFER OR HAVE AVAILABLE. WE THINK ALMOST EVERY VEGETARIAN WOULD ENJOY A DISH SUCH AS THIS, BUT IS CAN ALSO BE SERVED AS AN ACCOMPANIMENT TO GRILLED CHICKEN, MEAT OR FISH. **Serves 6** (V)

**4 ounces onions, finely chopped**

**4 tablespoons unsalted butter**

**2 1/8 cups Arborio or other risotto rice**

**5 cups vegetable stock, boiling**

**salt**

**7 ounces mushrooms, quartered**

**7 ounces zucchini, sliced about 1 1/4 inches thick**

**3/4 cup shelled fresh peas**

**7 ounces (about 3 1/2 cups) broccoli florets**

**5 plum tomatoes, peeled and seeded**

**1/2 cup grated Parmesan cheese**

**5 tablespoons unsalted butter, chilled and diced**

To garnish:

**fresh herbs such as chervil, parsley, basil or cilantro**

**grated Parmesan cheese**

In a heavy-based pan over medium heat, gently cook the onions in 3 tablespoons of butter until soft and transparent. Stir in the rice and stir gently for about 2 minutes. Reduce the heat to medium and add a ladle at a time of the vegetable stock. Stir fairly continuously and wait each time until nearly all the liquid has been absorbed before adding more. After about 15 to 20 minutes, the rice should be cooked and all the liquid added and absorbed. Check and season to taste with salt (vegetable stock cubes can be very salty, so taste before seasoning). Set aside.

Melt 1 tablespoon of butter over medium to high heat and gently fry the mushroom and zucchini. Strain into a colander, season with salt and reserve in a warm place.

Bring a pan of water to a boil, add the peas and broccoli florets, return to a boil and blanch for 1 minute. Drain. Arrange them on a baking sheet with the tomatoes and heat through in a hot oven or in a microwave for about 1 minute on medium power.

Stir the Parmesan and 5 tablespoons of cold diced butter into the risotto. Add all the warmed vegetables and stir to distribute evenly.

To serve, scoop onto warmed plates and serve immediately. Garnish with fresh herbs if desired and pass around an extra bowl of freshly grated Parmesan.

# Salad of Herbs

FRESH HERBS LIBERALLY SPRINKLED THROUGH SALAD LEAVES GIVES A WHOLE NEW DIMENSION TO A SALAD.

**Serves 4 to 6** 

**7 ounces mixed salad leaves**

**1 1/3 cups chopped fresh herbs such as chives, chervil sprigs, flat-leaf parsley sprigs, tarragon**

**3 to 4 tablespoons Standard Vinaigrette (see page 178)**

Simply sprinkle the herbs over the salad leaves, then toss the leaves in the vinaigrette and serve immediately.

# Buttered Apples
## on Sugar-Glazed Barmbrack

BARMBRACK IS THE IRISH EQUIVALENT OF A LOAF-TYPE YEASTED FRUIT CAKE. BRIOCHE WOULD BE A WONDERFUL SUBSTITUTE, BUT A GOOD-QUALITY WHITE LOAF WOULD BE FINE, TOO. SWEETENING THE CREAM AND FLAVORING IT WITH A DASH OF VANILLA EXTRACT MAKES A DELICIOUS CHANTILLY CREAM THAT IS PERFECT WITH THE BARMBRACK. **Serves 6** (V)

**1 loaf barmbrack, fruit cake or white bread**

**1/2 cup unsalted butter, softened**

**2/3 cup confectioners' sugar, sifted**

**1 1/4 pounds cooking apples**

**juice of 1 lemon**

**2/3 cup unsalted butter**

**generous 1/2 cup superfine sugar**

**2 cups whipping cream**

**few drops of vanilla extract**

Preheat the broiler to high.

To prepare the barmbrack, slice the loaf into 1/2-inch-thick slices. Either cut the crusts off and have a neat rectangle shape, or use a large pastry cutter and cut big rounds. Spread both sides of each piece with the softened butter and evenly sprinkle on some of the confectioners' sugar. Set aside.

Peel and core the apples, rolling each in the lemon juice to avoid discoloration. Halve and cut each half into 4 even wedges.

Heat a large heavy-based frying pan over medium heat and add the remaining 2/3 cup butter. After it has foamed, toss in half the sugar and stir constantly until it turns a nice medium caramel color. Toss in the apples and cook over medium to high heat for about 5 minutes, stirring and turning continuously, until the apples are a rich golden hue and can be pierced easily with a fork. If you don't have a large frying pan, cook in two batches to ensure even cooking and proper coloring of the apples. Remove the pan from the heat.

Place the buttered and sugared slices of barmbrack under the preheated broiler and watch closely. You just want an even golden toasting. Turn over and glaze the other side in the same manner.

Whip the cream until it holds fairly firm peaks, then fold in the remaining sugar and the vanilla extract.

To serve, place the glazed barmbrack onto warmed plates and spoon a generous portion of the buttered apples on top. Scoop a dollop of the cream on top and serve immediately.

# Mushroom and Eggplant Tart
## with Garlic Chives

THE RICH FLAVORS OF MUSHROOMS, EGGPLANT AND A LITTLE GARLIC HERE ARE SIMPLY DELICIOUS. HOWEVER, THIS IS A VERY VERSATILE TART THAT CAN BE USED AS A BASE RECIPE: SIMPLY CHANGE THE VEGETABLES WITH THE SEASONS. GARLIC CHIVES ARE AVAILABLE IN MOST ASIAN MARKETS. FOR A DELICIOUS LUNCH FOR FOUR PEOPLE, SERVE THE TART WITH THE SALAD OF HERBS (SEE PAGE 169). **Serves 6** (V)

**8 ounces Savory Pastry (see page 177)**

**3 tablespoons unsalted butter**

**7 tablespoons olive oil**

**12 ounces button mushrooms, quartered**

**salt and freshly ground black pepper**

**14 ounces eggplants, cut into 1/2-inch dice**

**2 tablespoons snipped fresh garlic chives or 3 garlic cloves, chopped**

**3 eggs**

**3 egg yolks**

**2 cups light cream or half-and-half**

Preheat the oven to 350°F. Grease an 8-inch tart pan with a removable bottom.

Roll out the pastry and use it to line the prepared tart pan. Place in the refrigerator to chill for at least 20 minutes. Cover with foil, fill with weights and bake blind in the preheated oven for about 10 minutes, or until light golden brown. Remove the foil and weights and set the tart aside to cool.

Reduce the oven temperature to 300°F.

In a large frying pan heat the butter and 1 tablespoon of oil until foaming. Add the mushrooms and fry until cooked. Season with salt and pepper and tip into a large bowl. Heat the remaining olive oil and fry the eggplant with a little salt over medium-high heat. Don't be tempted to add more olive oil, as this will make the whole dish too oily. Fry the eggplants until light brown and cooked through. Add the eggplants to the mushrooms and mix in the garlic chives or garlic.

In a medium bowl, whisk the eggs and egg yolks together until well blended. Add the cream, 1/2 teaspoon of salt and a pinch of pepper and whisk gently until you have a smooth mixture. Stir in the mushrooms and eggplants. Gently pour the filling into the pastry shell and cook in the preheated oven for about 40 minutes, or until the tart is completely set. Allow to cool for 10 minutes before serving.

# Penne
## with Broccoli, Goat Cheese and Sun-Dried Tomatoes

WITH A SATISFYING RECIPE LIKE THIS ONE, WHO NEEDS MEAT? THE TOMATOES AND THE CHEESE MAKE IT RICH AND FILLING, WHILE THE BROCCOLI ADDS TEXTURE AND VARIETY. TRY SUBSTITUTING OTHER VEGETABLES SUCH AS ASPARAGUS OR FENNEL. **Serves 6** (V)

**1 1/4 pounds penne**

**1 1/2 pounds broccoli florets, cooked**

**11 ounces (1 1/2 cups) sun-dried tomatoes in oil, drained and chopped**

**9 ounces fresh goat cheese, rind removed if necessary**

**3/4 cup virgin olive oil**

**salt and freshly ground black pepper**

Bring 5 quarts of salted water to a boil in a large pan. Add the penne and cook until just al dente. Just before you drain the penne, add the cooked broccoli florets, wait for 15 seconds then drain into a colander.

Return the pasta and broccoli to the hot pan and add the tomatoes, cheese, olive oil and some freshly ground black pepper. Check and adjust the seasoning to taste and serve immediately on warmed plates.

# Kiwifruit Soup
## with Passion Fruit Ice Cream

THIS LIGHT, TANGY DESSERT WITH ITS CLEAN, BOLD FLAVORS AND COLORS IS REALLY REFRESHING. A LEMON SORBET COULD BE SUBSTITUTED FOR THE ICE CREAM, WHICH WOULD MAKE IT A VERY LOW-FAT DESSERT OPTION. FOR A RICHER ICE CREAM, REPLACE HALF THE MILK WITH WHIPPING CREAM. **Serves 6** (V)

**1/2 cup passion fruit juice (8 to 10 fresh passion fruits)**

**2/3 cup superfine sugar**

**2 cups Vanilla Custard Sauce (see page 181)**

**12 fresh kiwifruits**

**juice of 2 lemons**

To get the juice from the passion fruits, halve each fruit and scoop all the flesh and seeds into a small pan. Warm gently with 2 tablespoons of sugar. This helps to release the flesh from the seeds. Pass through a fine sieve, pressing the seeds hard to release all the juice and flesh. You should have about 1/2 cup juice. Keep any extra to drizzle over the finished dessert and keep some of the seeds to decorate with as well.

Stir some of the juice into the cooled custard sauce to taste. Remember to make it slightly extra tangy because freezing will diminish the flavor.

Freeze in an ice cream machine following the manufacturer's instructions, or freeze in a shallow tray, whisking every 30 minutes to break up the ice crystals while freezing.

Meanwhile, peel the kiwifruits and place them in a blender or food processor with the remaining sugar and the lemon juice. Purée briefly. If it is left turning too long, the seeds will start to break up, discoloring the purée to a muddy brown. Pass through a fine sieve. Return a spoonful or two of the seeds to the purée and taste for flavor. There should be about 2 cups of purée. Chill in the refrigerator.

To serve, pour a generous ladle of the soup into each soup plate. Place a scoop or two of the passion fruit ice cream in the center and drizzle with a dash of passion fruit juice. Decorate with a few passion fruit seeds scattered over (they're totally edible).

OVERLEAF:

Meatless Meals, Menu 2

Mushroom and Eggplant Tart with Garlic Chives (page 171)

Penne with Broccoli, Goat Cheese and Sun-Dried Tomatoes (page 172)

Kiwifruit Soup with Passion Fruit Ice Cream (page 173)

CHAPTER SIXTEEN

# Basic Recipes

These are useful basic recipes that you will need for several of the dishes in the book. They will also come in handy at other times when you are cooking.

## Note on Baking Blind

Many recipes call for blind baking a tart shell. This is simply a prebaking of the shell. It is accomplished by lining the pastry with parchment paper or foil and filling with weights of some sort. This holds the pastry in place until it has cooked enough to be set. The pastry is cooked with this blind bake in place for about 15 minutes at 375°F. Often, after removing the beans and foil, the tart base is popped back into the oven for a minute or two to ensure that the bottom is evenly cooked to a golden brown.

A tip is to lightly brush the base and the sides of the cooked pastry with egg yolk to seal the pastry. This is especially helpful when the filling is a runny type, like the Lime Tart on page 29.

# Shortcrust Pastry

THIS IS A VERY WORKABLE SHORTCRUST, NOT TOO SHORT, YET CRISP AND TENDER. IT IS HIGHLY VERSATILE AS YOU CAN USE IT FOR ALMOST ANY RECIPE, WHETHER SWEET OR SAVORY. IT'S WORTH MAKING IN THE QUANTITY BELOW AND THEN FREEZING WHAT YOU DON'T USE THE FIRST TIME AROUND. **Makes about 2 pounds** (V)

**6 cups pastry flour**

**3/4 cup superfine sugar**

**1 1/2 cups (12 ounces) unsalted butter, chilled and diced**

**3 eggs**

**dash of salt**

Here, this pastry is made by hand, but it can also be made by pulsing in a food processor. Place the flour and sugar in a chilled bowl. Add the butter and rub it in until the mixture is pea-size consistency. Stir together the eggs, pour into the bowl, add the salt and mix until the mixture comes together.

Transfer the mixture to your work surface and, using the heel of your hand, work the mixture until it all holds together in a cohesive ball and there are no big lumps of butter unmixed. Divide into four even batches, wrap well in plastic wrap and chill. This pastry will keep in the refrigerator for about a week and in the freezer for about 1 month.

# Savory Pastry

SAVORY PASTRIES ARE THE BASE FOR SO MANY DISHES THAT IT'S REALLY WORTHWHILE TO PRACTICE WORKING WITH A SHORTCRUST DOUGH UNTIL YOU HAVE IT UNDER CONTROL. **Makes about 2 pounds** (V)

**3 cups plus 2 tablespoons all-purpose flour**

**2 tablespoons superfine sugar**

**2 teaspoons salt**

**1 1/2 cups (12 ounces) unsalted butter, chilled and diced**

**2 eggs**

**2 tablespoons whipping cream**

Here, this pastry is made by hand, but it can also be made by pulsing in a food processor. Place all the dry ingredients in a chilled bowl. Add the butter and rub it in until the mixture is pea-size consistency. Mix together the eggs and cream. Pour into the bowl and mix until the mixture comes together.

Transfer to your work surface and, with the heel of your hand, work until the mixture holds together nicely. Divide into three portions, wrap well in plastic wrap and either chill or freeze. The pastry should be chilled for at least 1 hour before being used. This allows the butter to firm up and the flour to relax.

# Standard Vinaigrette

YEARS AGO PEOPLE USED VINAIGRETTES TO DRESS SALADS AND SALADS ONLY. BUT NOW, REALIZING THAT THEY ARE TASTY, HEALTHY AND OPEN TO ENDLESS VARIATIONS OF FLAVOR, ONE FINDS THEM ON VEGETABLES, PASTAS, FISH DISHES, AND SO ON. A GOOD RATIO TO WORK TO IS ONE PART VINEGAR TO FOUR OR FIVE PARTS OIL. KEEP ALL VINAIGRETTES IN THE REFRIGERATOR IF THEY ARE NOT BEING USED IMMEDIATELY, OTHERWISE THEY CAN DEVELOP A RANCID TASTE. **Makes about 1 cup** (V)

**1/2 teaspoon salt**

**1/2 teaspoon freshly ground pepper**

**2 teaspoons Dijon mustard**

**2 to 4 tablespoons white wine vinegar**

**scant 1 cup olive oil or vegetable oil**

Dissolve the salt, pepper and mustard in the vinegar in a bowl. Whisk in the oil, slowly at first to allow it to be incorporated. Check and adjust the seasoning to taste. This can easily be made in a blender or food processor. Simply place all the ingredients in together and blend.

# Creamy Dill Dressing

A very simple and refined sauce for salads or fish, this goes very well with Smoked Salmon Salad Extravaganza (see page 20) or Salmon Terrine (see page 94). The sauce will keep for about two days in the refrigerator. If you are making it ahead, don't add the dill until the last moment or it will discolor. **Makes about 1 cup** (V)

**4 tablespoons lemon juice**

**2 teaspoons Dijon mustard**

**1/2 teaspoon salt**

**1/4 teaspoon freshly ground white pepper**

**1 1/4 cups whipping cream, chilled**

**3 tablespoons chopped fresh dill**

In a small bowl, whisk the lemon juice, mustard, salt and pepper. Stir in the cream and chopped dill.

# Pastry Cream

THIS PASTRY CREAM IS VERY THICK. REDUCING THE FLOUR OR CORNSTARCH WOULD LIGHTEN IT, BUT FOR OUR PURPOSES IN THIS BOOK WE NEED A THICKENED ONE. IT IS USED TO FILL ALL KINDS OF PASTRY DESSERTS FROM ÉCLAIRS TO PUFF PASTRIES TO TARTS. ITS VERSATILITY MAKES IT INVALUABLE IN DESSERT MAKING, SO PASTRY CREAM IS ONE TECHNIQUE THAT MUST BE MASTERED. **Makes about 3 cups** (V)

**2 cups milk**

**1/2 vanilla bean, split lengthwise**

**scant 2/3 cup superfine sugar**

**6 egg yolks**

**1/4 cup all-purpose flour, sifted**

**3 tablespoons cornstarch, sifted**

**confectioners' sugar (optional) to dust**

Place the milk and vanilla bean in a pan and bring to a boil over medium to high heat. Set aside to infuse.

Whisk together the sugar and egg yolks until they are light and pale yellow. Whisk in the flour and cornstarch and continue to whisk well until smooth.

Slowly pour some of the hot milk onto the egg mixture, whisking continuously. Pour in the rest of the milk and whisk to combine.

Return it all to the pan and cook over medium heat, whisking continuously, for about 2 to 3 minutes, or until the mixture comes to a boil. Continue to whisk continuously and let it cook for another 2 minutes. This ensures that the raw flour is cooked. Remove from the heat.

Strain through a fine sieve into a clean bowl. The vanilla bean can be removed at this stage, as most of the seeds will already have been released into the pastry cream. Either cover with a layer of plastic wrap pressed directly on top of the pastry cream or heavily dust the top with confectioners' sugar. Either method helps prevent a crust from forming while cooling. When cool the pastry cream can be stored in the refrigerator for up to 5 days.

# Vanilla Custard Sauce

SIMPLE VANILLA CUSTARD SAUCE, OR CRÈME ANGLAISE, IS AN ESSENTIAL RECIPE FOR ANYONE INTERESTED IN PASTRY AND DESSERT MAKING. YOU CAN BUILD VARIOUS FLAVORS AND SPICES INTO THIS BASE RECIPE. MOST, LIKE COCONUT OR CINNAMON, ARE INFUSED IN THE MILK BEFORE THE CUSTARD IS MADE. BUT REMEMBER, ALCOHOL AND HONEY SHOULD BE ADDED ONLY AFTER THE CUSTARD HAS BEEN COOKED AND COOLED SLIGHTLY. THIS CUSTARD CAN KEEP IN THE REFRIGERATOR FOR UP TO 5 DAYS, DEPENDING ON HOW FRESH THE MILK WAS TO START WITH. **Makes about 2 1/2 cups** (V)

**2 cups milk**

**1/2 vanilla bean, split lengthwise, or 1/2 teaspoon vanilla extract**

**6 large egg yolks**

**scant 2/3 cup superfine sugar**

Place the milk in a pan with the vanilla bean and bring to a boil. Set aside to infuse.

Whisk the egg yolks and sugar together in a bowl until lightened in color and the sugar has dissolved. Whisking continuously, slowly pour the milk into the yolk-sugar mixture and whisk together. Pour this mixture back into the pan and cook over low heat, stirring continuously with a wooden spoon, until the mixture has thickened enough to coat the back of the spoon and will hold if you run your finger along the middle of the back of the spoon.

When it is to desired thickness, strain through a fine sieve and let cool. You can leave the vanilla bean in the anglaise to continue to increase the flavor or remove it at this point, scraping all the seeds from the inside of the pod into the custard.

# Brandied Apricot Sauce

THIS SAUCE CAN BE KEPT FOR UP TO 2 WEEKS IN AN AIRTIGHT CONTAINER IN THE REFRIGERATOR.

**Makes about 1 3/4 cups** 

**about 8 ounces good-quality dried apricots**

**juice of 1 lemon**

**2 cups water**

**1 cup superfine sugar**

**7 tablespoons brandy**

Place the dried apricots, lemon juice, water and sugar in a pan. Bring to a boil and let simmer gently for about 30 minutes, or until the apricots are very soft. Remove from the heat and leave to cool slightly.

Purée in a blender or food processor and pass through a fine sieve. Taste to check sweetness/tartness and add the brandy.

# Black Currant Sauce

**Makes about 1 3/4 cups** 

**9 ounces frozen black currants, thawed**

**5 tablespoons water**

**2/3 cup superfine sugar**

**1 to 2 teaspoons lemon juice**

Simply place all the ingredients in a blender or food processor and process. Pass though a fine sieve and taste for flavor. Adjust with more sugar or lemon juice as necessary.

# Chocolate Sauce

HERE IS A SIMPLE CHOCOLATE SAUCE THAT'S EASY TO WHIP UP AND KEEPS VERY WELL IN AN AIRTIGHT CONTAINER IN THE REFRIGERATOR FOR A WEEK TO 10 DAYS. YOU CAN FLAVOR IT WITH A LIQUEUR IF YOU WISH.

**Makes about 2 cups** 

**2/3 cup milk**

**1/4 cup whipping cream**

**9 ounces bittersweet or semisweet chocolate, finely chopped or grated**

Bring the milk and cream to a boil. Remove from the heat and leave to cool slightly. Stir in the finely chopped chocolate. Stir until well mixed and all the chocolate has melted.

To reheat the sauce, melt in a bowl over a pan of simmering water, or at about half power in the microwave for 1 to 2 minutes.

# Toffee Sauce

A MULTIPURPOSE TOFFEE SAUCE WITH A REAL BUTTERSCOTCH FLAVOR, THIS GOES WITH SO MANY THINGS IT IS EXCELLENT FOR ANY PASTRY CHEF'S REPERTOIRE. THE SAUCE CAN BE USED WARM OR COLD. IT KEEPS WELL IN THE REFRIGERATOR FOR UP TO 2 WEEKS. **Makes about 1 cup** (V)

**2/3 cup firmly packed light soft brown sugar**

**1/2 cup whipping cream**

**2/3 cup unsalted butter**

**1 teaspoon vanilla extract**

Bring all ingredients to a boil together in a pan over medium to high heat and cook for 2 minutes, stirring continuously. The color will change to a rich golden hue. Remove from the heat and leave to cool.

# Index of Recipe Types

TITLES IN ITALICS ARE VEGETARIAN RECIPES.

## Starters



## Main Courses

### Fish and Shellfish



### Poultry and Eggs

### Meat



### Game



### Pasta



### Vegetarian Dishes



### Salads



### Buffet Dishes and Snacks

### Vegetable Side-Dishes



### Desserts



### Cakes and Breads



### Sauces and Dressings



### Pastry

# Index

PAGE NUMBERS IN ITALICS REFER TO THE ILLUSTRATIONS.